Thomas Schirrmacher

Modern Fathers

World of Theology Series

Published by the Theological Commission of the World Evangelical Alliance

Volume 13

Thomas Schirrmacher

Modern Fathers

Neither Wimps nor Tyrants

Translated by Richard McClary

Edited and Revised by Thomas K. Johnson

WIPF & STOCK · Eugene, Oregon

Wipf and Stock Publishers
199 W 8th Ave, Suite 3
Eugene, OR 97401

Modern Fathers
Neither Wimps nor Tyrants
By Schirrmacher, Thomas and McClary, Richard
Copyright©2019 Verlag für Kultur und Wissenschaft
ISBN 13: 978-1-5326-9607-7
Publication date 9/12/2019
Previously published by Verlag für Kultur und Wissenschaft, 2019

Contents

I. Children love Fathers – Fathers love Children

I. A Crisis and an Opportunity

Fatherhood in upheaval

It is an old myth which is not becoming any truer as it ages: Men were not made for children, because child-rearing is a woman's thing. On the other hand, what is actually correct is the following: Fathers and children are made for each other! There is nothing which can fulfill a man more than successful fatherhood! For that reason, this book will above all have to do with the opportunities social upheaval offers fathers.

I stood there with a friend after a worship service, conversing, and we both had our little children on our arms. An older woman came to us and said: "Gosh, you have it good, and your children have it good!" In the conversation which developed she told us that as a mother she had earlier been convinced that children had better not be left alone with men. If she had to go to the hospital, she gave her children to relatives and not to the father. This was not only due to the fact that the father worked. Rather, and above all, it had to do with worries she had about the child. Her husband, however, did not protest against it. He considered himself incapable. Of course, in the case of an emergency he could deal with the child, but in the normal course of things they were better placed with a female relative. Nowadays, in her opinion, she knows that it was a mistake to keep the children away from their father, and she is glad to see that younger fathers have it simpler nowadays.

But do they really have it easier nowadays? According to a study by the Institute of Social Research in Frankfurt, 65% of all fathers are more or less insecure. Germany's Family Ministry has presented similar results. For that reason, women write books such as *Mr. Undecided: Why Men are not good for Anything* (English translation of the title)[1] but have little to offer other than complaints. "The self-image of many men and fathers has become brittle. They no longer know what they should think of themselves. In the case of many, the insecurity is papered over with professional achievements or is suppressed by fleeing to distractions. And yet it noticeably gnaws at the understanding men have of themselves! . . . All this blurring of the male ego is the result of a long history of atmospheric disturbances ... For two centuries the conception of who fathers are has been devalued,"[2] such that fathers' efforts are less and less appreciated in society.

"Last century's incipient women's movement and its resuscitation at the end of the 1960s has led to profound changes in patriarchal social structures. As necessary as this revolutionary upheaval was, in like manner the polarization of gender has escalated, in particular by modifications to the traditional family. Within the framework of the liberation movement of men and women, the consequences for children have practically fallen out of focus. The serious problem of the increasing disintegration of the family constitutes a definitive loss of fathers for millions of children growing up."[3] In particular, since the principle of "irreconcilable differences" in divorce law has come to be dominant, there are thousands of children who are automatically awarded to their mothers (up to around 1850 they were automatically and likewise unjustly awarded to their fathers!). Fathers are frequently largely deprived of their rights but have to continue to supply the means of living for the children. The number of children who are children of divorce and are growing up without fathers reaches into the hundreds of thousands. It is time that fathers to be "equally entitled" and not automatically denied any capacity for child rearing. In a peculiar way, there is namely an encounter between the old division of roles (the man working outside of the home with no responsibility for child-rearing while the woman cares for the children) and feminist thoughts (the man is guilty of everything and had better keep his hands off the children).

At the same time, European Union Family Ministers are calling for fathers to take on a more active role in caring for children. They are calling upon companies to provide more latitude to parents and to fathers. This is, they maintain, also in their own interest, as the most qualified talent, in the form of fathers, often drains off: "Europe needs its fathers."[4]

Parents have to arrange and decide much more with each other today than they used to. Hardly anything is prescribed. The number of possibilities in all areas of life has increased enormously. When in the process the tasks and roles as father and mother are completely unclear because traditional and (post-)modern role models are mixed, misunderstandings, dissatisfaction, and contention are predestined to arise.

Recognizing the opportunities

It is actually nothing other than rehabilitating what it means to be a father. Of course, while doing so, it cannot be a matter of reviving the dictatorial picture of a father or of reducing the father to the function of a breadwinner. No, it is a matter of fathers fulfilling their responsibility to provide for and to protect, and it is a matter of fathers carefully but assertively introducing children into the world and having them mature into self-reliance.

For 200 years the meaning of fathers has all too often been played down, talked down, viewed as superfluous by science, or depicted as dangerous. And yet, that has changed nothing about the fact that an involved, loving father, as well as good social standing on the part of the father, has opened more opportunities in life than anything else. Thus, it is necessary not only to complain but rather to see that as a good opportunity for fathers! Most female Nobel Prize Laureates were encouraged by their fathers from the time they were small. These fathers believed in them and encouraged them in their research.

In this book what matters to me is to not to look at the crisis of fatherhood but rather to look at the big opportunities for fatherhood involved when having to and being permitted to rethink through tasks fathers face. "Never before were the opportunities so great for fathers to themselves define their roles and tasks according to their individual abilities and strengths (together with their partners)."[5]

I agree with Ian Banks: "As far as taking care of children is concerned, life for a father used to be much simpler. Simpler, but less satisfying."[6] For that reason, I would like to say the following to all men who are uncertain as to whether they want to enter into the adventure of fatherhood, or if they are already fathers but balk at complete commitment: "If you count yourselves among the unwilling or undecided fathers, then make yourselves aware that every charity organization of significance and name which works with children unrelentingly emphasizes the decisive role of the father and of his relationship to the children. The research findings of a number of acutely intelligent people shows that a child in school can demonstrate significantly better performance, and has a more positive attitude towards learning, if a loving father is available. It is not surprising that specialists are of the opinion that sons with fathers who participated actively in the rearing of their children had a more stable sense of self worth as sons than sons whose fathers were mostly absent."[7]

For me it is not a matter of continuing the ongoing patriarchal and feminist dispute, for there is rarely anything good which is born of insoluble conflicts, and surely not for children. Also, it is more devastating for the children when parents are continually arguing about their roles than when they choose one or the other division of tasks, are then satisfied about the roles as they have been divided up, and support their partners in such roles. Again, I agree with Ian Banks: "Look here, friends. It is not a war. Forget the battle of the sexes. We do not ask of women to conduct the Battle of Waterloo. We just have an inkling that it could be more fun to truly take care of children than it is to just create them."[8]

What this book should achieve and what it is not meant to achieve

To a certain extent, I have excluded women in this book, i.e.: Only occasionally am I giving advice to mothers with respect to their husbands. As a general rule, I am addressing fathers.

I have also refrained from repeatedly emphasizing how important a loving mother is for the development of their children. This is due to the fact that literature on this topic is a dime a dozen. I also do not want fathers to take up their roles in the place of mothers. And I am all the more not saying that I would like a world without women. It is not good when only men determine how the world goes, for as one can read in the first pages of the Bible, they are often helpless. God, who alone is our true "help" (Psalm 38), has declared: "It is not good for the man to be alone. I will make a suitable helper for him" (Genesis 2:18).

The book is nevertheless for women who live together with their husbands because there are not only many fathers who lack orientation. Rather, there are also many mothers who no longer know what they should expect from their husbands as fathers and what they should not expect.

Apart from that, this book is not a marriage guidebook, although it will also have to do with how strongly the relationship between the partners decides whether one is a good father. The difference between a man and a woman, which is essential for our topic, can only be addressed briefly.

I am writing this book a) as someone who has been reading the relevant literature on the topic of international research on fathers for many years, b) as an individual who counseled families over long periods of time and has thus seen and heard a lot from close proximity, and c) as someone with experience as a father who works from home and for that reason has had the fortune and privilege of witnessing from close proximity how both of his children are growing up and as someone who has had the fortune and privilege of shaping their upbringing – thus being a "modern father."

What I have written here is what I myself try to live out. Whether that has truly been achieved and is being achieved is something my children will have to judge in ten years. Some self-criticism befits every father, and as a Christian I am well aware of my shortcomings. In the end one does not become a Christian when one says: "God, I thank you that I am not like other men ... (Luke 18:11). Rather, one becomes a Christian by the plea: "God, have mercy on me, a sinner" (Luke 18:13). Being a father includes being able to acknowledge one's own failures and one's own guilt before one's children and obtaining forgiveness from God and the children.

One might make the claim that – as in my case – talk is cheap for two professors as parents with two children. Naturally, I do not want to prescribe my lifestyle to others, but I would at least like to say this much: We committed ourselves to our children before we were professionally successful and still have the firm rule that the children, even as teenagers, should never lack our care. We have either taken them with us on trips, or one of us has stayed at home. There have only been two times when we needed a babysitter for a half-day because we were traveling at the same time. This commitment which we ourselves made to be present at home has meant that many times it has led to giving up certain things professionally, but it has enormously stabilized our family life and has above all shown me fatherhood from a completely new side. Regarding this, I would like to repeat a piece stemming from an interview in 1999.

From a Christian Point of View: "Papa & Co." (Interview conducted in 1999)[9]

The most formative witness of a Christian, which I read about during my studies, is the witness of the prominent Methodist theology professor Lawrence O. Richards, who was confronted with the drug addiction of his daughter at the height of his career and had to acknowledge that due to the global service he had conducted he had neglected his family. Forgiveness and a radical restructuring of his life in which his wife and his children had top priority was also used by God in his grace to help the daughter out of her quagmire.

My spiritual fathers – my own father as well as, for instance, Francis Schaeffer, Rudolf Bäumer, Alfred E. Stückelberger, and Francis Nigel Lee taught me early that the most effective spiritual service has its roots in an intact and abiding marriage and family. In addition, we have received counsel along the way, especially in full-time service, to free up some time for small children since this time can never be repeated. Also, the time the children do not always want to be with mom and dad comes fast enough.

Therefore, my wife and I were in agreement from the very beginning that our marriage always had to have top priority, which often served as a lifeline and an oasis of tranquility. In order to plan time with the children, we became self-employed and made sure that our principal work – for whomever – could be done from the study next to our home. That also made it simple for my wife to be professionally active without tearing the family apart.

Just as I was to receive my first professorship after years of beavering away and teaching in the USA and my wife was to receive a guest professorship, which we accepted a year later, our son David announced his arrival. David's birth was one of the most uplifting spiritual experiences of what was not exactly a boring life and was only later matched by the birth of our daughter Esther three years later. God had created new life and entrusted it to our hands. The special birthing clinic in Bensberg, in which birth is given to a child as if one is at home, and where the couple enjoys absolute priority, allowed us to be entirely alone after the birth. We were so fascinated that for an hour we forgot whether we had a girl or a boy!

But now comes the oath of disclosure: Years of dreamed about plans were replaced by reality. Above all, my wife's and my being completely overtired due to too little sleep at night will remain unforgettable for me.

We decided that my wife would be there two-thirds of the time and I would be there one-third of the time for the children. In this way, my wife would have some "breathing room" to continue to conduct her research relating to Islam part-time and I would have time every day to really experience time with my children, to be there for them, and to raise them as a role model and not only as a voice from the background.

Have I ever regretted the decision? Could I have made more home visits and trips all around the world, been on more boards, and had more peace? Yes, for sure, and sometimes one thinks more about what one could still do. By the way, this can also be the case when one does not have children and is already operating at the limits of what is possible.

Now surely it was and is often strenuous to have time for the children and to reconcile that with my profession as a pastor, author, publisher, and theology professor. It is often exhausting. However, is it not that way, anyway? Is the only alternative seeing my wife have even more stress?

No, I have not regretted having a lot of time for my children in the middle of the chaos. And much less have my children and my wife regretted it! The close relationship to my children, talking about anything and everything, singing together, playing, and being silly is something I would not miss for the world.

Due to the emotional relationship, I gain stability for myself and ensure that my life does not rationalistically atrophy. My children force me to learn a lot and to have a look at things I have not occupied myself with for years. I understand more deeply that people and their love for each other and not things and concepts make up the creation. However, I also see my sins in a mirror, my mistakes and weaknesses, which I unwillingly pass on to my children.

"Dad, why did God make this butterfly red?" Indeed, why? "Dad, why are those construction workers not wearing helmets, even though the police want them to and it is dangerous not to wear one?" Yes, why? My children teach me to again pose completely simple – and often so difficult – questions. My children teach me how simple love is. They teach me how natural it can be to live with God, the cross, the Lord's Supper, and miracles. Every day they make me endlessly thankful to God. And they make me thankful to God for my parents and for all the time that they invested in me. And finally, my children love me with all their hearts, and that . . . does me good . . .

On the history of fatherhood

Families are continually changing as history marches on. When looking over the course of history, one does not find *the* picture of what a family is. There were times when as a matter of course mothers gave their children away to a wet nurse and parents let their children wander through the world as apprentices at the age of 12 or 14.[10] The role of the father has also greatly changed over the course of history and in various cultures.

Let us take a moment to compare the situation in the 18th century to today. Back then, there were hardly any institutions which were in competition with fathers, not the school, not the employer, not the media. This is because the family was the place of economic activity. There was nothing like the nuclear family as a private, protected space; one lived in large living communities, and the life expectancies for parents and children were short. One had godparents as surrogate parents who could jump in at any time. "Beginning in the 18th century, the mother took over many of the tasks which earlier were for the father. They became the house manager and responsible for child-rearing. This corresponded to increasing separation between homes and the places of fathers' employment. For their part, the mothers were released from contributing to the material support of the family through their own work. Initially, however, the de facto effectiveness of this only developed in the civil servant, academic, bourgeois intelligentsia, and aristocratic class. It is there that one meets the intimate private family, which gives much attention to its children and opens up the best possible educational opportunities. By way of contrast, family life does not play a leading role when looking at small farmers, craftsmen, and the later industrial proletariat. Mothers and fathers have to earn their livelihood by working, whereby children are felt to be a burden and are left to themselves. Children are integrated into the labor process as early as possible."[11]

Roughly speaking, if one looks at the focus of development – reality was naturally much more differentiated, and changes happened regionally and in different social strata in a quite varied manner – the following periods of time can be distinguished:

Up to 1800: The family is an economic unit of production, with the father as its leader. The wife is for the most part significantly younger than the husband and mostly does not live very long. As an independent factor within the larger common household, the nuclear family is still hardly identifiable.

1800-1850: The beginning of the dissolution of the family as a unit of production, whereby income is increasingly generated outside of the family. Wedlock is increasingly considered to be a protected, private space for values and feelings. The father is above all the moral advisor and planner for the professional and family future of the children. In the case of a divorce, he automatically receives the children.

1850-1900: Through industrialization, the family finally loses its role as a unit of production, and the father increasingly becomes a provider working outside of the house and spending 18 hours per day away from home. As a consequence, alcoholism becomes a problem for fathers. The new bourgeois status symbol with respect to the working class and the lower class is that the wife does not work. Children leave the parental home at an early age.

1900-1960: The father is above all the provider for the family and the moral role model. Since the 1920s, the father has above all spent time together with his children for leisure activities (e.g., sports activities). The period of education becomes longer, and children remain longer in the family. In the 1930s to the 1950s what emerges is the "ideal image of the father as a protector, breadwinner, and disciplining individual for the family."[12] However, he does not take part in the care and supervision of the children. The separation between breadwinner and the caring role into male and female tasks has not been as strong as that at any time prior or any time since.

Excursus from a Christian Point of View: Authority between a Softy and a Tyrant

How are we as Christians to deal with changes in our society? How are we to judge the 1968 revolution and how did changes move us from a situation where there was a traditional nuclear family to a situation where there are 'colorfully' diverse family forms? The questions can be asked in another way: Is there a certain father image which is deemed to be ethically Biblical or Christian and can and must serve as a standard?

Christians are neither automatically conservative no are they automatically progressive. *They do not want to conquer today's spirit of the age with yesterday's spirit of the age.* They know from Paul's call in Romans 12:1-2 that an individual can only avoid conforming to the pattern of this world if prepared and able to be continually changed through the renewal of his or her thinking and by never stagnating in examining the will of God. There one reads: "Do not conform any longer to the pattern of this world, but be transformed by the renewing of your mind. Then you will be able to test and approve what's God's will is – his good, pleasing, and perfect will."

Christianity is very conservative when it comes to the preservation of God's order of creation. However, it is very progressive and revolutionary when it comes to surmounting false traditions and unjust rules, which wrongly claim an absolute status such as God's commands. A pure conservatism in order to pacify the older generation is as foreign to the Bible as is mere change for the satisfaction of the younger generation. Whoever as a Christian, for instance, feels strongly about lifelong monogamous marriage out of love and obligation and thinks that children need a mother *and* a father as a point of reference, is counted in Germany as a die-hard. At the same time, however, in Saudi Arabia, that individual is a revolutionary who wants to unhinge the time-honored culture.

Whoever nowadays seeks to practice Christian ethics should not allow himself to be defined according to a scheme that is either "conservative or progressive," that pursues "restoration or revolution," or that is "past-oriented or future-oriented." Christian ethics should not be allowed to be grist for the mill of the spirit of the age or of Evangelical Phariseeism.

A good example is the 1968 revolution in Germany and similar things that happened in other Western countries. These events placed all forms of authority into question. Not everything prior to that was good, but it is also the case that not everything before that was bad. Conservative Christians tend to romanticize earlier days, and progressive Christians tend to demonize them. However, whoever thinks in terms of the Bible, cannot allow himself to be pressed into such a mold. Christians are happy about those points where the 1968 Revolution toppled immoral authorities or brought about the collapse of bourgeois facades. Christians regret those points where Biblical values were destroyed. Because Christians believe in creation, in which God set the state and parents as the highest authorities, they have never been able to straightforwardly endorse anti-authoritarian child rearing. However, does that automatically mean that what was practiced prior thereto as authoritarian child-rearing was straight forwardly correct and that there was nothing worth getting rid of? Was not the penchant for draconian and violent punishment sometimes too unbridled? Was parental authority not all too often viewed as unlimited, without judging whether it served the goal of the well-being of the child? And were not children all too often treated according to fixed formulas without taking their differences into account? Apart from all the negative side effects, has it not also been a benefit of modern pedagogy that every child is seen as an individual and that education is to be adjusted to every child? For Christians, all of that was actually already prescribed in the Bible by the fact that authority never exists for its own sake. Rather, it has always been given by God for a certain, precisely defined purpose and is to be measured against the good for which he gives it. And has God as Creator not made children so diverse and endowed them with gifts and abilities of all sorts?

In light of the frequent failures of authoritarian upbringing in the past and the failures of anti-authoritarian upbringing in the present, what is it that Christians have to offer instead? What differentiates a Biblical orientation from both of them? Judeo-Christian anthropology (the study of humankind) exists in a certain tension. On the one hand, humankind is created as the "image of God" and endowed by God with unbelievable abilities and various possibilities. On the other hand, as a "sinner," humankind has turned from God and is capable of unbelievably evil thoughts and actions. On the one hand, the evil in the world can only be addressed by containment and submission, and on the other hand by forgiveness and grace. Accordingly, developing self-sufficiency, on one hand, and integration and obedience, on the other, form a closely related set.

For this reason, Christian pedagogy lives on the basis of a thoroughgoing complementariness. Children are viewed as images of God needing direction and encouragement so that the abilities they have been given by God can unfold. These abilities can be artistic and literary as well as interpersonal. An independent personality under the Creator is the goal of child rearing and education. Education is not an end in itself. Rather, it targets a time in which the individual to be educated is able to take on complete responsibility for his life.

Children are likewise seen as people, who, owing to sin, no longer live according to their original intention and for that reason need to be educated away from evil; this includes boundaries and punishments as much as it does counseling, assistance, and gracious pastoral care. Christianity is in this regard very self-critical and very critical and mistrustful since it assumes that every individual not only allows himself the occasional blunder now and then. Rather, in normal everyday life, every individual is characterized by egoism which injures oneself and others.

All too often, authoritarian child rearing lost sight of the fact that each child is an unmistakable and distinct personality created by God and that the goal of every form of child rearing is healthy self-reliance. The Bible itself sees leaving the parental home at the age of about 20 (in the Old Testament the age of legal majority, of the ability to direct and defend oneself) to be the normal situation. Authoritarian child rearing all too often placed the holder of the office in an absolute position without measuring himself against the one for whom he received his authority. Authoritarian child-rearing assumed too often that if one had driven evil away or had limited it, then something good had been achieved. Authoritarian child rearing was too often an end in itself, one in which the father had a right to be served after a strenuous day and that to obey was of value in itself. This is the only way to explain that the army was praised as the "school of the nation" with its oft brutalizing tendencies – it only was a matter of obedience per se.

The 1968 generation, then, built upon an all the more extreme pedagogy of "the good in humanity" and thought that this goodness would develop on its own. All that had to be done was not to stand in its way and exterminate all authority. Suddenly authority itself was evil, and setting limits no longer served to protect against what was wrong and to learn the good and the useful. Rather, it was made out to be sinister. The old insights of experience, which said that whoever was raised in a good and intensive manner is often later a more self-confident person with backbone, while the contrary of little supervision in childhood leads to unsure and manipulatable adults, have been lost.

Christian child-rearing builds upon a pervasive complementarity: law and grace, encouragement and boundaries, self-reliance and leadership all belong together. Whoever only sees the "positive" side as the program education is to follow will be brutally overrun by evil in child-rearing (and likewise in school). Whoever only sees the "negative" side declares child rearing and punishment to be ends in themselves and loses sight of the goal. Children need boundaries[13] as well as freedom to develop.

The following illustration applies to each type of authority but can be understood most quickly if you look at it with respect to child-rearing, no matter whether one is thinking as a child about one's teacher or whether one is thinking as an educator who is himself in charge of children.

Three Types of Authority

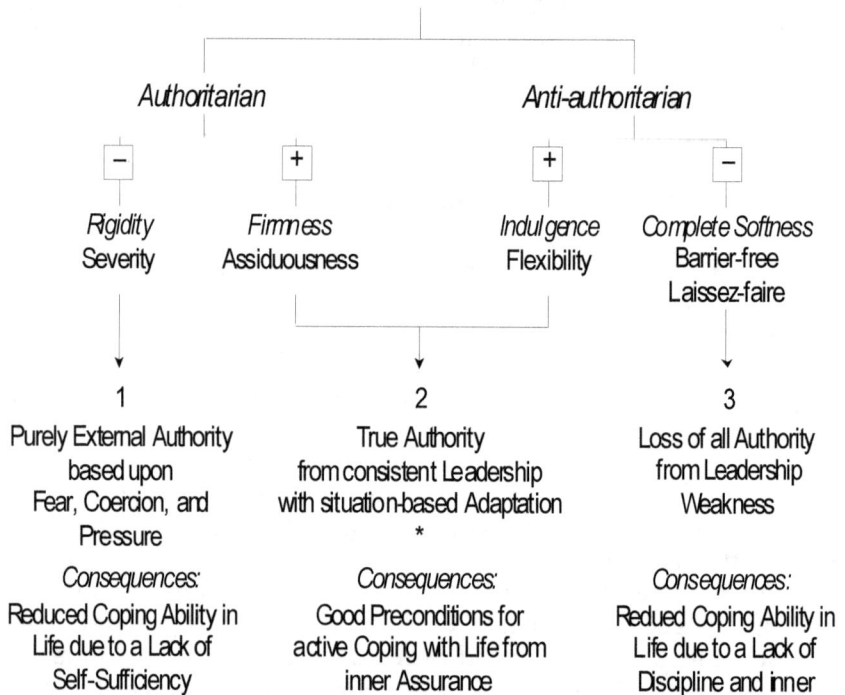

Authoritarian		Anti-authoritarian	
−	+	+	−
Rigidity Severity	Firmness Assiduousness	Indulgence Flexibility	Complete Softness Barrier-free Laissez-faire
1	**2**		**3**
Purely External Authority based upon Fear, Coercion, and Pressure	True Authority from consistent Leadership with situation-based Adaptation *		Loss of all Authority from Leadership Weakness
Consequences:	*Consequences:*		*Consequences:*
Reduced Coping Ability in Life due to a Lack of Self-Sufficiency	Good Preconditions for active Coping with Life from inner Assurance		Redued Coping Ability in Life due to a Lack of Discipline and inner

Biblical complementarity should really be evident to every individual from experience, whether that person is a Christian or not. We all know how uncomfortable superiors are who are as tough as nails and do not factor us in as people or, on the other hand, those who never want to commit. We all know that we ourselves would not have wanted parents who always said no, nor would we have wanted those who always said yes. We all know that our children expect real authority from us as well as a completely individual form of love and encouragement. We all love neither sergeants nor tyrants, neither softies nor "Mr. Indecisiveness."

Let us take a concrete example for how fatherhood is lived out. And how the times change! 90% of all fathers are present at the birth of their children and easily count as loveless if they do not want that. As recently as the 1970s, it was not even desired in most hospitals, or it was even forbidden to be present at the birth. Being present at the birth as a father was the exception. In 1992, I still had to have a discussion in order to be able to be at the birth of our first child. Also, in order for this to happen, we had to change hospitals. But is this change something which a Christian has to fight only because it used to be different? Of course not! The birth of a child is one of the most precious goods and to take part in it can be a real spiritual experience and can lead the husband to come to a new sense of astonishment regarding who God is.

2.   The Comeback of the Father in Father Research

Infants love fathers – fathers love infants

Michael E. Lamb, the founder of father research in the USA, wrote the following back in 1976: "For the first time, there is documented evidence that many fathers enter into an intensive interrelationship, that the type of relationship differs from that between mothers and infants, and that infants do not demonstrate a consistent preference of one parent over the over. There can be little doubt that the father is often an important person in the life of the infant and of the young child."[14] The second leading American father researcher, Henry B. Biller writes similarly: "Researchers have found out that even in the first years of their lives, a strong bond to the father can be built. These bonds are clearly reflected in the reaction of the infant to the behavior of the father. Thus, for example, infants who have a bond to the father spend much more time looking at their father and actively reacting when their father comes in the room or leaves the room, and they often produce movements indicating their desire to be close to their fathers. The extent of such a bond to the father stands in intense relationship to the quality of the fatherly engagement with respect to the infant."[15] And finally a third quote from the great America father researcher, Michael E. Lamb: "It is extremely important to remember that one of the most influential characteristics of the father-child relationship appears to be their warm and tender manner."[16]

Naturally, this should not minimize the significance of the mother for the infant. Lamb comes to the explicit conclusion: "Infants who have two positively involved parents tend to be more curious and more eager to explore than those who do not have a close relationship to the fathers. As a general rule, they deal more maturely with strangers and react more competently when it comes to complex and novel forms of stimulation. Infants with a good relationship to the father are more certain and more trusting in the expansion of their explorations, and they can be somewhat more advanced in crawling, climbing, and handling objects."[17]

Kyle D. Pruett of Yale University, in his book *Fatherneed*, brings together the reasons why a child needs the care of a father as urgently as he does that of his mother:[18] "Development research clearly shows that children are born with a drive to find their fathers and to bond with them, and fathers have the internal ability, an instinct, to be responsive to this. Children and fathers hunger for each other very early, often, and for a long time."[19] A bad or a missing relationship between the father and the child damages the child as well as the father!

It has been known for a long time that motherhood, from the time of conception up to the time of weaning and beyond, is strongly hormonally regulated. Only recently has it come to be known that in fatherhood there is likewise a hormonal control mechanism which is triggered by pregnancy and birth. However, this can also become engaged through looking after small children, also as a result of non-biological, social fatherhood,[20] thus for instance in the case of a stepfather. "For a short time it has been known that expecting fathers experience hormone swings completely similarly but with less amplitude. Their hormone levels fluctuate considerably and rather closely track the pattern of the pregnant woman. Various studies additionally showed that up to 65% of all first-time fathers experience distinct symptoms of pregnancy: tiredness, a boost in appetite, mood swings, and headaches. Many experienced psychological roller coasters and fall into depression – which might also have to do with the fact that during the pregnancy men have at least as many concerns about the future as women do. Normally, once the child has arrived, there are strong emotional bonds the father immediately establishes that are as strong as the mother's, and he is just as competent in dealing with the child. Ross Parke, a leading father researcher at the University of California, has conducted extensive observations of fathers with newborns in laboratory situations and at home. They speak just as much with their babies, kiss them just as often, play with them as long as their mothers do ... In reaction to a crying child, the heartbeat rises in

the case of women as well as in men, as do blood pressure and skin tem-
perature, while they remain unchanged in the case of a smiling baby . . .
'With the exception of nursing, there is no indication that women are
biologically predisposed to being better parents.' This is Michael Lamb's
conclusion."[21]

The devastating influence of scientific theories

How was it possible that such knowledge remained unknown for so long
or was suppressed? "Child rearing is a woman's thing!" With this established wording, a number of individuals have brought about a circum-
stance where for most inhabitants in the West it is above all the mother
who is seen as being of vital importance for the welfare of the child. Naturally, children first of all mostly go to the mother after a divorce. If a
child is going to be raised by one of the parents, then it is better that it is
the mother rather than the father, isn't it? And many fathers have surely
not even been angry about the fact that they had less and less of the responsibility for raising the child.

    Therefore, it is no wonder that the mother-child relationship stood in
focus in connection with child rearing and with the development of the
child. While there are thousands of works on the role of the mother in
the development of the child, the father-child relationship has seldom
been the object of investigation.

    There is hardly an area where parroted fundamentalist scientific the-
ories, which have never actually been proven, have had such a devastating effect as in the area of fatherhood. Whoever had another opinion was
muzzled as being unscientific, whereby we know today that much of
what was held was only wishful thinking.

    American father research has lodged a protest since 1975. It was in
1985 that Wassilios E. Fthenakis first criticized numerous schools of psychology[22] which held a one-sided emphasis on the mother for scientifically substantiated. He came and still comes to the result that the primacy of
the mother for the development and the raising of the child is not a scientific fact. Rather, it is ideology. Inge Seiffke-Krenke, a psychology professor from Mainz, aptly breaks down father research into three phases.
In the first phase the father was seen as distanced and superfluous. In the
second phase he was measured against the mother and, for that reason,
was considered to be deficient. It was not until the present third phase
that fathers have come into their own: Fathers simply deal differently
with children.

The first false dogma is John Bowlby's "bonding theory": The child bonds only to one person and not to two, i.e., there is a tie to the mother. The father is for that reason superfluous in the initial years.

"The father was viewed as irrelevant for the emotional development of the infant and small child . . .," which "in the meantime has shown itself to not be scientifically supportable.[23] Investigations have shown, for example, that two-year olds can themselves have a good relationship to the father[24] if they have a bad relationship to the mother and that children can also have an exclusive bond to the father if no mother is there.

This bonding theory does not even apply to the animal world. In the wake of Konrad Lorenz, Bowlby maintains that young animals and human children only develop the closest relationships to a single living being, mostly the first one they catch sight of.[25] As far as Fthenakis is concerned, this theory is not only disputable. Rather, it has also never been demonstrated with respect to humans. On the contrary: All investigations point out that an emotionally balanced development which leads to true self-reliance on the part of a child implies a close bond to two individuals of different genders and that the father can likewise become an intensive bonding person for the child.[26]

Why were only those animals always chosen as models for which the father was not a participant in the rearing of young animals? Why not emperor penguins, sticklebacks, herring gulls, ostriches, and seahorses? Or, if one prefers to take primates as examples, why not South American titi monkeys or marmosets (tamarins) where the father performs hard labor in jointly rearing the young animals, or even those types of animals where the father raises the young animals alone, such as emus, kiwis, or wolves?[27]

The second false dogma is the Freudian teaching on the *Oedipus Complex*. According to Freud, the child initially only needs and desires his mother, and the son experiences the father as a rival in a battle for the mother in the "Oedipal phase" between the third and fifth years of life. This, in Freud's view, leads to fears of castration. The small boy wants to marry the mother and kill the father.

In 1976, Michael E. Lamb determined what the devastating consequences were of Sigmund Freud's view, which up to the present day have often been dogmatically defended but have not been established by any evidence.[28] "If the psychologist *Lenzen* spoke of the dissolution of the father in the 20th century, then it was psychoanalysis that provided the theoretical framework by perpetuating the thesis of the exclusivity of the mother-child relationship."[29]

To sum it up, one can agree with Horst Petri, a professor for psychotherapy and psychosomatic medicine: "It is a simple fact that within the framework of the men's and women's liberation movement over the last decades the consequences for children have been either practically dismissed or justified by ideologically colored arguments which have in the meantime been shown to be gross fallacies ... How could thing go so far that in times of peace and general affluence fathers endlessly break from their responsibility for their children or are systematically marginalized by mothers? Far too few are slowly waking up from this situation to a nightmare which has become reality."[30]

Children have a good influence on men

Let us take a look at modern father research beginning with how men profit from fatherhood before we ask what children gain from their fathers. Many studies have shown that fatherhood has a positive influence on men. On average, men in Germany who have children drink less alcohol than their childless equals, show anti-social behavior less frequently, and have a lower crime rate.[31] For example, in *The Economic Journal*, George A. Akerlof examined the difference between men without children and those who lived with children. According to official statistics in the USA, in 1991 the crime rate of childless men was significantly higher than that of married men with children. In prison there are 2.6 men with children per thousand between the ages of 18 and 44 and, in contrast, there are 17.6 men who are unmarried and childless per thousand.[32] As a main reason for the difference, researchers see *commitment* and the attentiveness fathers have for the family leaping from one area of life to another.[33]

The fact is that "parents are almost as strongly altered by their children as children are by their parents,"[34] and that the responsibility which a man with children carries causes him to concentrate on wisely using his energies, thus transferring this mindset from the family to other areas of life. Horst Petri, for instance, is of the opinion that a man needs a profession and family in order to direct his strong male drives of aggression and and sexuality into socially correct channels so that they can have a positive impact.[35]

The consequences of fatherlessness

Now back to the question but stated the other way around: Do children need fathers? Samuel Osheron, a psychologist at Harvard, writes: "The psychological or physical absence of fathers from their families is one of the greatest underestimated tragedies of our time."[36] Horst Petri writes the following on this: "It is high time to acknowledge the catastrophe related to fatherlessness."[37] And one of the leading American father researchers wrote the following decades ago: "To the degree that society does not support a constructive role of the father in child rearing, it pays a price in the form of rampant individual behavioral disorders, of the disappearance of valuable abilities, and different types of social problems. A very large number of children, in households with two parents or only with mothers, are victims of chronic neglect by the father. Deprivation of the father is often linked to personal insecurity and weak self-confidence... In our society, there is only a small probability that children who do not have a close relationship with their biological father will receive constant attention from some other male adult."[38]

It is time to hold a brief for fathers! Fatherlessness damages the psychological, physical, and cognitive development of children. The scientific arguments for this have long since been amassed, since the end of the 1970s, but have been undesired in politics and the media. "A critical analysis of the available empirical studies shows that there are certain development and personality disorders that have to be counted on in the case of children who grew up fatherless. Their causes, however, lie not only in the loss of a father or in the prolonged absence of a father. Rather, it is co-determined by the adverse effects of the living environment and of the social relationship patterns of the child."[39] One of the first forms of media coverage which drew intensive attention to it in Germany was the news magazine *Focus*: "In two articles dating from 1995, a dramatic picture was sketched. The first, entitled 'Where is Dad?', carries the subtitle: 'The Trend to Single-Parent Homes is Unbroken. The latest research shows: Children without a Father have it distinctly more difficult in life.' ... 'Over one-third of the children suffer from serious psychological problems. Almost two-thirds of all rapists, three-quarters of juvenile murderers, and a similarly high percentage of all prison inmates grew up without a father.' Fatherless children tend to demonstrate more failure in school, more drug addiction, and more socially conspicuous behavior. Girls are more often the object of sexual abuse, and as teenagers get pregnant more frequently. The implication: 'After it became chic to rationalize fathers away as machos and power seekers, as insensitive, as workaholics, as shying away from things having to do with the household and therefore a figure which is dispensable for the child's room, they have suddenly been discovered by research as VIPs and as particularly important people.'"[40]

Later in *Focus*, Ulrike Plewina wrote the following: "As victims of the divorce boom, more and more children are growing up in a practically 'manless' society, at least without a stable male role model. Stepfathers can hardly replace a biological father. Elfriede Mittag, the Chairperson of the Association of Cities and Towns for the federal state of Northrhine Westfalia, additionally sees a real deficiency in the 'purely female living environment of kindergarten and elementary school.'"[41] Gender equality? Where are the men in elementary schools and day care facilities? More and more children are growing up in a world without adult male role models. Should we not have long since introduced a men's quota into the care of children and adolescents?

The Düsseldorf professor for psychosomatic medicine and psychotherapy, Matthias Franz, has discussed "epidemiological findings on the meaning of early absence of fathers for the psychological health in later life" in *Zeitschrift für psychosomatische Medizin* (translation of the journal title: *Journal of Psychosomatic Medicine*).[42] He has formidably documented the negative consequences increasing fatherlessness has for our children, which has been caused due to absent fathers, due to the loss of the father due to divorce, and due to a situation where the mother is the single parent from the very beginning.[43] He writes: "While the meaning of the loving and present mother for the development of a small child is not open to reasonable doubt, the importance of the father does not appear to have been recognized to the same degree. In the course of this, children of divorce experience a heightened risk of poverty, psychological disorders, dropping out of school, later unemployment, delinquency, and early pregnancy. For example, as adults they have a heightened risk of suffering from psychological disorders and psychosomatic illnesses. In particular, in the case of patients with depression, anxiety disorders, or aggressive impulsive types of behaviors in male adolescents and adults, various studies described the absence of a father during the years of childhood development."[44] In short: "Children who grow up without a father, are

- 5 times more likely to commit suicide;
- 32 times more likely to run away from home;
- 14 times more likely to commit rape;
- 9 times more likely to quit school at an early age;
- 10 times more likely to take drugs;
- 9 times more likely to end up in a reform school;

- 20 times more likely to find themselves in prison;
- 33 times more likely to be seriously physically abused;
- 73 times more likely to be the deadly victim of abuse."[45]

In his book *Das Drama der Vaterentbehrung* (English translation of the title: *The Drama of being Deprived of a Father*), Horst Petri has impressively documented the consequences of growing up without a father.[46] At the same time, he can point to a variety of scientific studies from all sorts of subject areas. "The influence that being deprived of a father has on intellectual abilities can be verified in achievement tests, school results, professional qualifications, and in professional success. In research there is far reaching agreement regarding the negative effects of father deprivation."[47] Studies in the USA, Sweden, Japan, China und Korea[48] confirm Petri: "If the father is home a lot and participates fully in child-rearing, thus himself at times being the only one conducting the child-rearing, the children involved achieve a clearly higher intelligence quotient and are happier."[49] "Overall, research results suggest that the availability of a male role model in the home environment are of foundational importance for the development of specific cognitive abilities in middle childhood and for success in school as well as in allowing there to be a forecast of self-confidence in one's ability to perform."[50]

Protection against mistreatment and abuse

True fatherhood also ensures that children are more protected against mistreatment and sexual assault. It should be made clear that research focused too long on violent fathers and often the impression was given that fathers, owing to their masculinity, were dangerous per se for children and were significantly more dangerous than mothers. Those who abuse children are, statistically seen, only very rarely the biological father and especially not those who are personally strongly involved in care and child-rearing. Rather, if it is at all a question of biological fathers, then it is those with a great amount of distance to their children or with severe psychological problems (e.g., addiction problems). On a statistical basis, however, it is more frequently divorced fathers, fathers without custody rights, stepfathers, or the mother's new boyfriend who is also living in the household, especially the less they actually have to do with the children.[51] In the leading work of research on this topic, one reads: "It is seldom the case that a father abuses a child with whom he developed a close bond in early childhood. On the other hand, a father who did not form a close parental bond demonstrates a greater probably of mistreating his child or passively allowing others to abuse the child."[52]

Fatherhood also protects the child from assault by others: "Positive engagement on the part of the father is a great advantage, for sons as well as for daughters. Effective fathering can help protect the child against mistreatment and against inappropriate mothering, by directly contributing to the emotional well-being of the mother as well as by sinking the level of stress for the mother by sharing the parental responsibilities. Mothers in families in which the father is deeply involved demonstrate a more limited probability of resorting to severe punishments, are less restrictive, and less overprotective. A child with a good father has, in all likelihood, the peace of mind and the assertiveness to resist inappropriate manipulation and mistreatment from the side of other family members. Effective fathering can also reduce the likelihood that the child will be mistreated by non-family members. A child with two effective parents exhibits a lower likelihood of susceptibility for manipulation and abuse by neighbors, teachers, or strangers. Compared with those children whose fathers are absent, such a child probably has a better developed sense of assertiveness and self-reliance … Furthermore, such a child is probably emotionally secure and able to communicate possible problems to the parents. On account of their thirst for love and acceptance, children who do not have an involved father have a greater likelihood of vulnerability for inappropriate advances from non-family members."[53] "Families where there is only one parent present a particular risk for child abuse. The daily pressure and stress on the single parent heightens the probability of child abuse (and also the likelihood of mistreatment of the parent by the child).[54]

Child abuse should by no means be played down at this point,[55] but the following applies: *The protective function of the father against violence and abuse has to be emphasized in the face of voices from the media that fathers are dangerous.*

Fathers and the gender of their children

Many studies have shown that the father also plays a central role in a child's building a healthy self-identification with their male or female gender. "The quality of an early bond with the parents is an important factor in the development of gender roles and of the character of the small child. The first two to three years of life can be decisive for the establishment of individual gender identity. Early deprivation of the father can endanger the attainment of secure gender identity, especially for boys. The absence of the father and other forms of fatherly insufficiency prior to the age of four or five years of age can delay early development into manhood. Even if the development of gender roles in the case of girls is not so directly affected by being deprived of a father as is the case with boys, an early history of fatherly insufficiency can entail difficulties which women later have in contact with men during the time of adolescence and adulthood.

> "On account of their influence on a child's identity and self-image in the early stages of life, functioning gender roles are very important for small children. A positive involvement on the part of the father helps to give a healthy start to the development of self-esteem, whereas indifference and mistreatment by the father leads the child to be particularly vulnerable to various types of gender-related difficulties. With regard to the comprehensive psychological adjustments, a solid gender identity and a satisfied acceptance of one's own sexuality are most important and not the degree of superficial manliness or femininity."[56]

Sexual promiscuity among children and the number of teenage pregnancies is statistically significantly higher without a caring father, and likewise the number of children who have a high degree of difficulty with their own gender.[57]

Fathers and daughters

For daughters, the father is generally known to be the first great love. For that reason, no one can spoil the love for men over a lifetime as much as the father, and no one can prepare a daughter so positively for one of the most beautiful sides of life as the father can.

Many women marry men who are astonishingly similar to their fathers, in good aspects as well as in bad aspects. Women often marry alcoholics if their father had a problem with alcoholism, even if they loathe alcoholism. A father who esteems and loves other people has a good chance that his daughter will choose someone as a partner who loves her and not someone who will destroy and burden her life. Cordes has written: "The absence of fatherly love has serious negative consequences for daughters, and these negative consequences are shown particularly clearly in the relationship to other members of the male gender."[58] For instance, this applies to eating disorders as well as to forms of depression.

In addition, one finds the following: "Fathers determine much more than mothers, what it means to be a 'girl' and whether she feels comfortable in her own feminine skin."[59] "Studies have ... shown that socio-emotional disorders in girls who were raised without fathers can be expressed in two ways, either in a certain anxiety, shyness, and insecurity towards male gender partners or in a tendency towards promiscuity and inappropriately direct behavior with boys of the same age and with male adults."[60]

Recommendations for fathers

- Give your children a joyful anticipation about fatherhood and motherhood. Speak positively about real fathers and mothers (for instance, you own parents or parents whom your children know).
- Talk very early with your children about smoking, alcohol, sex, violence and everything about which one *does not* like to talk. As soon as your child can observe something of this nature, it is time to explain it to him! If you do not do it, someone else will. Be the first person if possible, even if you think that it is too early!
- Speak about the pressure from individuals of the same age with respect to sexuality and other questions, and encourage your children to be independent.
- Make it clear to your children that sexuality and relationships with a partner are similar to school and education: Whoever thinks short-term may appear to be having a lot of fun now, but later there will be a lot of problems. Whoever thinks long-term does without now and invests, and in return has long-term advantages and happiness in life.
- Always help your children to set short and long-term goals. What else are they going to use to orient themselves?

Recommendations for fathers with daughters

- Tell your daughter that she is the daughter you always dreamed of. And hug her again and again.
- Tell your daughter repeatedly that you love her, but also that her true beauty is found in her inner values and her gifts and abilities.
- Teach your daughter to have self-respect. Encourage her in all of her abilities, also in those which surprise you or which others do not understand.
- You will shape your daughter with everything that you do and do not do, and with everything that you are or are not. Make sure

that your daughter does not view being a man as being grumpy, egotistical, aggressive, and uncontrolled and later associate this with being a man. Rather, make sure that being a man is linked with compassion, a willingness to make sacrifices, courage, loyalty, and consistency.

- Tell your daughter what men mostly do worse than women and when it is wise for men to listen to women.
- Always protect the privacy of your daughter!

Recommendations for fathers with sons

- Hug your son in the morning as a way of greeting him – and likewise when he comes home. Even 18 year-olds like to be hugged, even if they dispute it.
- Your son learns from your position as a role model that a readiness to help, courage, dependability, and honesty are good male characteristics, or he will probably not learn them at all.
- Tell your son that women can often confuse you, and tell him about their feelings, regardless of whether he wants to speak about his feelings or not.
- Tell your son about the devastating consequences of (sexual) infidelity for others and for oneself.

3.   The Indispensable Father

Triangulation – being independent of the mother through the father

Children need mothers and fathers. Specifically, on account of their bond to their mother, which arises from the time of pregnancy, birth, and breastfeeding, they need the father in order to become independent. If the child is one of three individuals with the parents (in Latin expressed as trias, thereby triangulation), then the child can be at a healthy distance to one of the parents with without losing safety and a sense of emotional security.

Who does not know the situation where growing children often shuttle back and forth from one parent to the other? While they shower one parent with cuddling, gifts, and compliments, they are sounding out the extent to which they can distance themselves to the other. We all need self-assurance as an individual as well as a sense for community, the ability to adapt to others, and the ability to independently say no. We all have to learn: "Love your neighbor as yourself."

"If the child seeks to turn away from the mother, but no one is there to receive the child, the child remains in a grip. The child instinctively feels threatened. Mistrust settles in. And this mistrust can determine the entire personality development; it can become a devastating disruptive element, which in the end even shapes the character of the individual."[61] Modern psychology speaks about a "triangulation phase" with respect to children between the first and third years of life. The child vacillates between its will to independence (autonomy) and a return to unity with the mother. The father plays a central role in this stage. The child is able to disengage from the mother without giving up his or her security. The child is able to move to a necessary distance from the mother while in the the arms of the father. "Mother and child need a father who is present. He protects the child from severe fears of abandonment and helps the child to give up the desire for symbiosis with the mother." In addition, the following applies: "The mother is more in a position to support the desire for autonomy on the part of the child and release the child if the child feels love and affirmation from the father."[62]

Furthermore, Petri writes: "In connection with triangulation, frequently a type of 'buffer function' on the part of the father is spoken of. This eases the child's surmounting of separation anxiety and ambivalence and accelerates detachment from the mother. A further factor is that the child has two separate objects of love in this triangular constellation at his disposal, the mother and the father. They offer two different identification possibilities, one feminine and one male. As a result, the child's maturation process is decisively driven forward."[63]

Children also "belong" to fathers

Children need both parents. Children "belong" to both parents. Whoever justifiably reluctantly employs the word "belong" and would rather speak about their being "entrusted" to us parents, the following applies: Children are equally entrusted to both parents.

That also means that the fact that the father is biologically less active in conception, pregnancy, birth, and the period of breastfeeding does not mean that he has fewer rights or obligations with respect to the child.

The statement "my womb belongs to me" is not only an inhumane statement towards the child in the womb of the mother. It is also inhumane towards the father. No, the womb with the child does not "belong" to the mother. It is entrusted to her in order to protect life, to nurture and to develop towards independence – and that always occurs together with the one who conceived this life in and with her and receives it as a gift from the hands of the mother.

If a mother shows herself to be undeserving or a father shows himself to be undeserving because the life of the entrusted child is being damaged, then intervention is allowed to occur. However, apart from that, both carry complete responsibility, regardless of how high their biological contribution was.

Men are different; fathers conduct child-rearing differently.

Children need fathers as much as they need mothers, but they do not need their father as a second mother. Children also do not simply need their fathers as a second caregiver. Rather, it is in his differentness that he is needed. Children do not just want more "mothering" from their fathers. Rather, they have expectations of their father, as the French psychology professor and perhaps most significant child researcher Jean le Camus has documented in detail in his two bestsellers.[64] For that reason, the leading father researcher Fthenakis comes to the following conclusion: "With their respective resources, father and mother make different and yet equally important contributions to the development of their child."[65] And for that reason the following applies: "To win fathers to be more interested in the concerns of the children and of the family will not be successful as long as fatherhood is understood as quasi a copy of motherhood."[66]

Kyle D. Pruett has written: "Fathers do not mother ... At the age of six weeks, infants can distinguish the difference between the voice of their mother and the voice of their father. At eight weeks they can decipher complex differences in the style of care and handling they receive from the mother and from the father ... And that is only the beginning. Children often speak their words (or their sounds) for 'father' earlier than they do for 'mother,' and no one really knows why. Does that lie in the fact that the mother and the child are so close that the mother does not need a name? Does it lie in the fact, then, that the somewhat more distant quantity which is the 'father' needs a name? At the age in which children are able to walk and speak, they can independently detect their own father."[67] The bond to the father is in no way less intensive than that to the mother. Probably, however, the basis of the relationship in the case of mothers and fathers is different, for both interact differently with the baby. Fathers take babies much more frequently into their arms in order to play and to frolic around, while mothers take them into their arms more frequently to feed them, diaper them, console them and to cuddle with them or to keep them away from undesired activities. These differences suggest that the mother-child bond and the father-child bond serve different functions: The mother serves as a source of calmness, security and safety when the baby is troubled and stressed. The behaviors of the father might show the baby how it can interact with its social environment."[68] "Diverse studies have shown that women primarily regulate the internal world of the feelings of children, that their manner of handling the negative emotions of the child (sadness, fear), for instance, is highly relevant for the child's future social behavior. Men, in contrast, regulate the more 'exploratory' aspect of development, the relationship to the world. That is to say that they regulate everything which makes children ready to come to terms with the demands of the environment. Fathers are artful experts at encouraging this curiosity and their children's will to persevere. They tend to encourage the child to try things which are unusual more than the mother does and expect more of them. Fathers put a child back on a bicycle after the child has fallen down. They use longer sentences with small children, more complex words, and less rhythmic sentence melodies … They are more persistent in teaching small children to endure frustration when learning."[69] "Family researchers have found out the following: The importance of the mother in child rearing has been largely overestimated. Without fathers, no offspring is correctly prepared for life." The following was ascertained at the University of Regensburg: "The delicacy of feeling the father has in playing, for instance with a two-year old, correlates very strongly and unambiguously with the bonding behavior children still have in the ages of 16 to 22. The more sensitively the father treats the small child, the more securely the child will deal with emotional bonds as a young adult. Still more: as adults, children rather precisely reproduce that behavior which fathers have demonstrated towards them when playing. If the father has been patient with the child, attentive to the child, and approachable by the child, then 22 year-olds are the same way to their partners. They trust them more, are more open, are emotionally more fulfilled and turn more often to fellow human beings for help and consolation. The children of insensitive fathers, in contrast, have far more problems in relationships with partners, are more reserved, and more mistrustful."[70]

Let us choose two classical examples which have already been mentioned and which have to do with the different styles of child-rearing exhibited by fathers and mothers. In the first instance: *language.* Mothers tend to speak with their children in a more childlike manner with a lot of ability to empathize. Fathers simply speak more directly, and they use more unknown and unfamiliar words. However, this is no longer only seen as a negative factor. While mothers primarily encourage understanding and language as means of conveying a warmer relationship, the father encourages the child to learn, reflect, and to grow beyond themselves. Here one finds that language is more powerfully a means to classifying his environment. Both are equally important for a child, but one cannot replace one by the other. Likewise, there is as little reason to mutually have a bad conscience about the differences as there is for the parents to mutually have a bad conscience on account of the things which they have in common or could have in common or where the pair apparently play reversed roles.

The difference continues into puberty. "As far as communication between adolescents and their parents is concerned, the verbal exchange with the mother is indeed more extensive, but conversation with the father is more frequently perceived to be more satisfying and more effective, in particular as far as discussions about various objective topics and approaches to solving problems is concerned. On the other hand, in the case of personal and emotional problems, it is primarily daughters who tend to seek to talk with, seek assistance from, and seek the advice of mothers. Additionally, adolescents of both genders demonstrate more intimacy in their conversations with their mothers. Daughters in particular experience communication with their fathers to be less satisfying than verbal exchange with their mother when it comes to the areas of feelings and relationships."[71]

Secondly: *Care and play which incorporate risk:*[72] Mothers are predominantly care-oriented with their children and are very concerned with their well-being. Fathers play more physically with their children, play more games with rules, and teach in a playful manner how to integrate oneself. In doing so, fathers are much more prepared to enter into risk and challenge the child to do things which it is actually not in a position to do. Fathers also feed children differently, mostly in a manner which is playful.

Who is not aware of such examples? Two fathers are throwing a child back and forth to each other, and the child is elated while the mother stands horrified. And who is not aware of such discussions between parents: The mother is – often for too long – troubled about the safety of her children. The father, on the other hand, lets the children run on a long, independent, and risky leash – often too early in life. Both are important, for the child thereby receives a feeling of security and safety as well as self-confidence and the experience of coming of age. However, the concrete decisions which are born out of such discussions are mostly more appropriate for the child than the view of the mother or the father on their own.

This has nothing to do with old clichés. Rather, it is the practical experience of many parents which confirms scientific studies: If children are planning something risky, they more frequently ask the father about it. If they are injured or are fearful, they more frequently go to the mother. Modern researchers on the topic of bonding see the role of the father as one who challenges, as one who is a mentor and protector of independence.[73]

Indeed, the term "protector" is used because which wife would not want her husband to place himself before her and her children and demonstrate courage? This is not a matter of a *John Wayne Syndrome*, the lone wolf who uses force to serve justice without regard for wife and family and other relationships. Rather, it has to do with a courageous husband who also risks his health out of love to his family.

Inge Seiffke-Krenke has condensed research results:[74] Mothers deal with babies more from a care-giving perspective (e.g., bathing, changing diapers), while fathers tend towards imitation games. They stimulate small children with sounds and optical stimuli. Later on, as children are growing up, fathers stimulate children with movement and sports and, in particular, in the case of sons, encourage autonomy and gender-specific role behavior. After puberty, they above all remain important contact individuals for questions relating to school, professional occupations, and political topics.

All of that should naturally press no one into a role or prohibit him from displaying the ostensible behavior of the other gender. Rather, it should bolster the individual in living out their own gender identity and in self-confidently and joyfully expressing it. Every father is father in a different way, and he should not be a father like his female partner nor in the manner his neighbor is a father nor in the manner the media expects him to be. "I do not want to say that fathers and mothers have to spend exactly the same amount of individual time with their children. How parents split up responsibilities in child-rearing depends upon the particular preferences and family circumstances. It is important, however, that the couple maintain a cooperative partnership and that the child perceive emotional involvement on the part of both parents. A child needs the opportunity to develop a highly qualitative individual relationship with the father as well as with the mother."[75]

Excursis from a Christian Point of View: Teaching Prayer and Conveying Values

If children learn to pray on a regular basis, then it is mostly from their mothers. But they tend to pray more over the course of their lives if their father prayed regularly and was a role model to them in his dependency on God. When the Bible summons fathers to speak with their children about God, and fathers do this, it first becomes clear to children that faith is also something for raw, everyday life.

The Institute for Economic Research has established the following: Whoever prays several times during the week has a reproduction rate of 1.9 children, while people who do not pray have, on the other hand, a reproduction rate of 1.3. Divorces are more seldom in the case of people who pray, and, in contrast, there is much more time available for marriage and family. Dependency upon God makes individuals fond of children.

An important request in the Bible also applies to child-rearing: "If any of you lacks wisdom, he should ask God, who gives generously to all without finding fault, and it will be given to him" (James 1:5). Children are free to notice that parents often do not know how to proceed and ask God and others for advice.

In addition, we have repeatedly noticed that children strongly orient their values throughout life towards the values of their fathers and seen why it is important that fathers live out these values in front of their children and often explain them by using concrete examples.

Raising children with and towards instilling values

1. Values are conveyed through trust:
"But as for you, continue in what you have learned and have become convinced of, because you know those from whom you learned it, and how from infancy you have known the holy Scriptures, which are able to make you wise for salvation through faith in Christ Jesus. All Scripture is God-breathed and is useful for teaching, rebuking, correcting and training in righteousness, so that the man of God may be thoroughly equipped for every good work" (2 Timothy 3:14-17).

2. Values are conveyed by example:[76]
". . . not lording it over those entrusted to you, but being examples to the flock" (1 Peter 5:3).

> *3. Values are practiced through rules*
> and
> *4. Time is needed to convey values:*
> "Love the Lord your God with all your heart and with all your soul and with all your strength. These commandments that I give you today are to be upon your hearts. Impress them on your children. Talk about them when you sit at home and when you walk along the road, when you lie down and when you get up" (Deuteronomy 6:5-7).
>
> *5. Values are conveyed through dealing with conflicts:*
> "Therefore each of you must put off falsehood and speak truthfully to his neighbor, for we are all members of one body. In your anger do not sin. Do not let the sun go down while you are still angry, and do not give the devil a foothold" (Ephesians 4:25-27).

Recommendations for fathers who want to "father" children

- Do not try to "mother" your children. Rather, bring self-consciously into the family that which corresponds to you as a man. In doing so, it is naturally not a question of what *the* husband or *the* wife would do. Rather, it is a matter of which strengths and weaknesses you bring along as the couple you are.
- Have trust in "common sense" and a healthy mistrust towards too much advice from science and the media. Together with your partner, find your particular style as father for a great number of years, and do not peer to much at that which is continually changing in the environment or at that which is expected of you in the media. "Children do not need parents who have studied the newest educational and psychological theories and are now utilizing techniques oriented towards those goals. Instead, the ability to dialog and demonstrate understanding are called for."[77]
- Listen and speak as much as possible with your children. Produce opportunities for this (e.g., individually take a day trip with each child).
- Children speak differently with fathers and use them as counselors and as a walking encyclopedia. Consciously take time for this, even if there is officially no problem pending. Go with your son into a cafe and ask him what he would generally like to ask you. Let yourself be told by your daughter what she thinks about her classmates.

- Be there at all times for your children, but even more importantly: Be there when it is important for your children! Whether children or other people or your profession have the priority, do not always make it dependent upon whether they have priority from the perspective of time. However, children have a fine sense for whether one jumps to deal with others and consoles them or just the opposite!

Brainsex

Naturally, the different styles of child-rearing by fathers and mothers also have something to do with the differences between men and women. Without ignoring the enormous range found within the genders, without ignoring the overlaps found between the genders, and without wanting to cultivate the old clichés of past centuries, all attempts to explain the differences between men and women as purely dependent upon the way one is raised prove futile.

Numerous studies of "modern" pairs and their children, where men and women have equal rights and where the mother is employed, have shown, for instance, that also in their cases there is very quickly a traditional division of child-rearing tasks and within the home (also in cases where the effort is equal from a time point of view). Men and women remain different, even if politics and science declare something else.

Anne Moir and David Jessel, in representing many other researchers in their book *Brainsex: The Real Difference between Men and Women*, have described that the differences between men and women are already very clearly seen in our brains.[78] The publisher describes the book as follows: "The differences between men and women are more vast than we suppose. This is due to the fact that their brains, and along with that their intellectual capacities, differ diametrically [= opposingly]. However, this does not lie in the society or in child-rearing. Rather, it is solely conditioned by psychological developments in the womb. The authors demonstrate, for example, that men are superior to women when it comes to areas of logical thinking, comprehending mathematical relationships or orientation within geographical space. On the other hand, women have a clear edge when it comes to intuition and emotions. Dealing with language is easier for women than for men. This is due to the fact that the center for language in the male brain is found in the left brain hemisphere while in the case of women it extends over both hemispheres of the brain. For the authors, it is not at all a matter of setting up theses which are misogynistic or to destroy achievements made by the emancipation movement. Instead, through precisely determined scientific facts they want to open a way to a new understanding of roles whereby everyone recognizes their abilities in order to meaningfully contribute them in some connection, through their professional lives, or in society."[79]

This is not the place to go into detail on these differences, and it is also not a matter of forcing someone into a role and, for instance, conveying the idea to a mathematically gifted daughter that her behavior is unfeminine. However, what it has to do with is not letting oneself be forced from the outside into being something one is not. An individual will not be happy if he is continually forced into a role socially, societally, and politically for which he was not created and which he cannot authentically and honestly fulfill.

The meaning of marriage for fatherhood

On the basis of studies, one finds successful father-child relationships most frequently where there is a harmonious long-term relationship between parents.[80] At the same time, the quality of the relationship between the pair and the quality of the relationship to the children have a close relationship to each other. "The ability of the husband/father to look after the children and to be sensitive is a key factor for a satisfying marriage as well as for successful relationships between parents and a child. Particular acknowledgement has to be given to the particular ways in which fathers and mothers share parental duties and can improve the development of the child. How parents divide the work in the family depends upon their specific circumstances; however, it is decisive that children perceive a constant sense of emotional engagement from the side of the father as well as from the mother."[81]

For this reason, parenting guides have long since spoken again about "the importance of a good marriage."[82] For instance, this is where the following is conveyed: Marital partners are the architects of the family and for that reason decide about the emotional environment in which children live. Psychologically healthy parents are good role models. If the marriage is good, the children find safety and security. The main this is that the elements of family life and the tasks of the father and the have been thoroughly discussed and clearly agreed upon. How these have been agreed upon mostly plays less of a role for the marriage and the children. A dialogical marriage is for that reason also a model for children of how various understandings are harmonized. Acknowledgement of individuality and harmony are thus simultaneously possible.

Mothers need the support of fathers

Included in the importance of the marriage for parenting is the mutual support and encouragement of the partners. "A number of the most important works of research with respect to the role of the father in the family system have to do with the ways in which the presence of the father and the quality of the relationship between the father and the mother influences and conveys the relationship between the mother and the child. There is much evidence that when fathers are supportive, mothers are more competent and respond better to infants and small children. Even prior to the birth of a child the presence of an emotionally supportive husband can contribute to a feeling of well-being in the pregnant mother and the probability of a relatively problem-free pregnancy and birth as well as increasing the probability of successful parenting . . ."[83]

Let us briefly summarize the results of research:

- Mothers demonstrate more interest in the care of their newborn baby (including nursing) when they receive a high degree of emotional support from the side of the father. The quality of the relationship between husbands and wives says more about the anticipated success of the mother in dealing with her child than any other factor.
- Mothers are more successful and more relaxed in setting limits and in the supervision of their two and three year old children if fathers are present in the situation. Children more probably comply with the requests of their mother than was the case without the presence of the father, even if the father was not directly involved in the situation. When fathers expressly support the requests of the mother, there is a particularly high probability that children will comply . . . The presence of the father reduces the number of motherly calls for control and simultaneously heightens the success of motherly disciplinary measures and the positive quality of motherly reactions when their children comply.
- Conversely, fathers also show more joy in caring for their infants when they receive encouragement and emotional support from their wives. Fathers with a good marital relationship and a positive view from the side of their wives are more probably involved in playing with their sons in infancy. Fathers who had stressful contact with their wives and perceive them negatively tend more

to only marginally engage in playful activities with their sons in infancy.

- Overall the following applies: Whoever has a positive family image is a more partner-like, more sensitive, more inviting, and wiser companion for his children.[84] And this positive family image is something he will mostly have brought from his own family of origin.

Recommendations of how fathers can support mothers

- Tell their children what a fantastic mother they have.
- Listen to and speak as much as possible with the mother of your children, and do that a lot when the children are there.
- Show your children that their mother is your number 1 and explain to them that you are going to still be together with "Mom" when the children have long since left the house.
- Depend upon the advice of your wife, who often knows better than everyone else, for instance, also better than doctors and teachers, about what is up with the children. Ask your wife on which occasions you absolutely have to be present in the life of your children (e.g., I am not allowed to ever miss my daughter's birthday party and my son would never buy a computer without me). Do not let it give you a bad conscience if your wife knows your children better than you. Women are most of the time able to read character and feelings more easily and better than men.
- "Children mostly learn to argue by imitation."[85] Discuss in an exemplary manner with your wife, thus in a manner that becomes clear that people have different points of view but at the same time in a manner that leads to a solution without losing respect for each other or giving up love for each other.
- Do not speak in a derogatory manner about your partner in front of others or in front of the children. Having a different opinion and having your partner stand there as incapable, dumb, superfluous, or egotistical are two completely different things!
- "Many fathers cannot envision how strenuous care and providing for a child can be. And many mothers are hardly able to pull themselves away from their child and do not know at all that their partners can care well for the child."[86] For that reason, husbands should by all means care for a child for a weekend by themselves and at the same time grant the mother some relaxation.

Fathers need the support of mothers

Conversely, the father also needs the same support of the mother. "If one views the beneficial and obstructive conditions for fatherly involvement, then the quality of the pair relationship becomes conspicuous as an important influential factor. Thus, there are hardly any fathers found who are living in an unhappy relationship with a partner and who participate strongly in the care and support of a child. This leads to various conclusions. First of all, those fathers who are heavily involved in care relieve their wives. Being occupied with the children is thus also motivated by caring for the relationship between the couple. However, what is more important is the function the mother has in initiating and configuring the activities the father has with the child. Many fathers apparently need the encouragement and guidance of their partner in order to become more strongly engaged with the child. This applies in particular when it comes to the ages when the child is an infant or a small child."[87]

Mothers should repeatedly bolster husbands' and call upon them to concrete tasks and convey to their children how happy they can be to have a father who is truly present and is involved. "More crucial is ... the attitude of the wife. If she denies her husband's competence to be able to appropriately care for the children, then he will hardly raise a finger. He can be as convinced as ever by his own skill – but if his wife is not taken by it, he will not move into action. Ross Parke, an expert from the USA, emphasizes the following: 'Fathers are precisely as involved as the wife allows.'"[88]

Recommendations for women who want real fathers as husbands

- Mothers, how can you be sure that your husband will be a good father? Above all: Make it clear to him that you want him to take a hand in things, to be present, and to make his children (able to) love him.
- Repeatedly and mutually discuss what you expect of each other and set down rules of the game so that both of you do not always have a bad conscience because you believe the expectations of the other are not being fulfilled.
- Call upon your husband to take concrete actions and fulfill concrete tasks (e.g., "It is time to speak with your son about kissing ...") and make it clear to him what has the top priority for you. Do not expect that he can come up on his own with what is to be done or what you expect. Men often get their wires crossed and are thankful if they get a concrete problem to solve.

II. Fatherhood in Light of Modern Problems

1. Fatherhood, Profession, and Career

Invest in the family as in education and career.

Günter F. Gross, a pioneer in management consulting in Germany dating back to 1953, wrote his most successful book in 1989. It was entitled *Beruflich Profi, privat Amateur?* (Translator's English translation of the title: *A Professional at Work but an Amateur at Home?*). So far, there have been 20 editions of the book published, and it has been translated into nine languages. He speaks to men who have successful careers but who are failures at home and in the family – if only because they are never there. Precisely for managers and others who work he sees "Opportunities for having a Happy Marriage" (the title of the first half of the book) if they apply the same skills in the family that they do in their work. He is brutally honest in revealing how much the family often only gets to run along at the margins, and the successful manager, however, deeply suffers as a result of this. Gross wants to impress upon the reader that quality of life encompasses all of life and not only the time spent in the company and that a foundational change of heart is not only necessary but also possible.

Whoever is a professional in investing should also be in the position of investing at home! Whoever does not invest does not earn anything! And whoever is a professional also knows that money is not the only thing to invest. Often it is also time, energy, interest, relationships, and ideas.

Today, many women make the mistake that they used to accuse men of making, namely of placing their profession and career above the family and the closest friendships. A true solution only first comes about when fathers and mothers mutually consider how they will grant their relationship and their family a long-term and internalized priority and nevertheless work towards their professional desires.

Both parents should especially take a lot of time for the toddler phase but also for adolescents in puberty. Why does one have to achieve everything in life just at the time when one has small children? Is there not a big before and after today, owing to long life expectancy? Are not the opportunities for part-time work and computer work from home a great chance for families nowadays? By the way, enough studies show the following: If the husband becomes a "househusband," the children can be cared for just as well. The difference is that he does things in a bit of a different manner than a "housewife."[89]

My parents are presently in their mid-80s. What they have left is what they have invested in their family. What many studies show is that older people with family on average live happier and look back with satisfaction on their life's work. Their professional life has long since become history. In light of present life expectancy, is it not "modern" to convey to my children that family is more important than career? For my children, family begins with their conception and ends with death. Their profession begins at 20-25 years after conception and currently ends statistically 20-25 years prior to death. Also in the time between, it is the situation within the family which still more deeply determines true happiness in life than anything else.

Uniting professional life and family remains a constant challenge. It is above all made difficult from the side of business, which would prefer to hire only singles. However, the performance and social competence of fathers and mothers is by all means appreciated by business and gets "frittered away." Franz-Xaver Kaufmann has written, "Even where entitled rights exist, for example in the case of parental leave or part-time work, the circumstances outside of public service are so constituted that it is practically not doable – by men even less so than by women! It is not so much the prejudices and arbitrariness of individual people which hinders it. Rather, it has to do with the structural idiosyncrasies of our economic system, which does not have any regard for whether employees take on parental responsibility or not."[90] "We are therefore able to speak of a structural social lack of consideration towards families."[91]

For this reason, it is gratifying to see that the Federal Ministry for Family Affairs, in collaboration with industry, started a nationwide initiative which in the meantime has found expression in many efforts called "local alliances for the family." This is where companies and municipalities are designing family-friendly workplaces and are calling for "family-friendly jobs instead of job-suitable families."[92] "Tying bibs and ties"[93] are possible, and model companies such as Hipp have developed excellent models for this and should serve as a role model for other companies. It should also embolden most fathers (and mothers) to call for similar measures in their workplaces.[94] Most fathers and parents have long since not exhausted everything there is which has to do with time-based, technological, and financial possibilities for making work more flexible and more family-friendly.

And yet compatibility is torpedoed by wrong language rules and common opinions. For instance, the following is wrong: You only work if you "have a job." Indeed, the fourth of the Ten Commandments says that you are to work six days, but where does it state that work has to occur in exchange for money? It is just as wrong when a mother's work is not acknowledged when she stays at home full-time for her small children as it is for the father or for the mother who leaves their place of employment early for the sake of their children and has to hear: "So, you're already calling it a day?"

The idea is just as wrong that children "become stupid" or antisocial at home. One should be honest enough to say the following: kindergarten, child day-care centers, nannies, and all-day schools above all benefit the parents and not the children. The current message of many of those who are "politically correct," that full-day care has to be expanded in order to strengthen education and children's social skills, is a self-serving declaration for the relief of parents and not a fact that has been documented in any way through experience, much less a fact which has been substantiated by science. Neglect of children – never, however, highly involved parents who are able to work out taking a lot of time for their children – produces children who are uneducated and not socially integrated! Since we nowadays have an increasing lower class in which children get into a bad state[95] and increasingly have incomplete families coming into existence, state alternatives are sensible. However, this is not the case because the state could be thought to even to some degree replace two highly involved parents for their children, and much less that the state could trump them.

Recommendations for reconciling profession and fatherhood

- The more love, time, and energy you invest in marriage and family, the more love, time, and energy you get back, now, soon, and all the way into old age.
- Bring your profession and extra-familial interests into your family and do not "privatize" your conversations at home – your children will appreciate being led to harsh realities and appreciate the fact that they do not have to get to know about these things in a completely surprising and ambush-like manner.
- Take your children as often as possible to your place of work and let them be there when you are practicing your profession. Children want to be proud of what their parents do. Additionally, they

will be able to experience that parents are subject to just as many constraints as, for instance, children in school and can learn how to deal with that. Children never ask more questions than when they are confronted with the everyday profession of their parents!

- "For the love of money is a root of all kinds of evil" (1 Timothy 6:10). Pay attention that money does not rule your relationships in your marriage and to your children. Money cannot secure or buy love, but one can entrust one's life to money and in the process lose love and relationships.
- Collect ideas about how you can better combine your profession and family. Is there the possibility of telecommuting, of part-time work, of flexible work hours? What is important in the process is the following: not what others think about you but rather finding a mutual solution in which one can completely support the other partner and does not feel like the sole victim.[96]
- For instance, make yourself clear when an important meeting in the company is set for 4:00 p.m. and you would rather have it in the morning.
- Discuss as a couple how you can alternate giving priority to your profession and your family. Whenever I was completing a doctorate, my wife took over practically all tasks at home. When she was completing her doctorate, I was responsible at home. We also never write books at the same time. When one of us plunges into such a task, the other is especially there for the children.
- Buy for your wife (and for yourself) the newest time-saving appliances for your household after you have closely observed your everyday life and have asked your wife precise questions. And learn how to use it yourself.
- Divide up the work in the household, from cooking to repairs, by first of all saying what 1. each of you like to do anyway and 2. what is not too much trouble. What really has to be broken down is what is left over, which both of you really do not want to do. When you divide up the work for the family, think about everything which takes a lot of time and energy and what costs a lot of nerves:
  providing care, feeding, cleanliness, repairs, dealing with the authorities, watching over the accounts, administrative work, relaxation, spiritual education, prayer, going-to-bed-rituals, etc.
- Give away work in the household rather than your children. Invest in a cleaning company instead of a day care center.

Excursus from a Christian Point of View: The Task of the Father in the Bible – Provider or Child-Rearer?

1. In the Bible it is the father and mother who continually – and who innumerable times are mentioned together – as mutually having the final responsibility for the raising of the children and share the work associated with this. It is almost without exception that father and mother are mentioned as role models, portrayed with authority and blessing, and more seldom only the father or the mother. A harmonious marriage is the best precondition for child-rearing because the husband and wife find fulfillment towards their children in an interplay wonderfully planned by the Creator.

Father and Mother in the Bible (Examples)

- "Honor your father and your mother, so that you may live long in the land the Lord your God is giving you" (Exodus 20:12 [= Deuteronomy 5:16]).
- "'Honor your father and mother' – which is the first commandment with a promise" (Ephesians 6:2).
- "Listen, my son, to your father's instruction and do not forsake your mother's teaching" (Proverbs 1:8).
  "When I was a boy in my father's house, still tender, and an only child of my mother . . ." (Proverbs 4:3).
- "My son, keep your father's commands and do not forsake your mother's teaching" (Proverbs 6:20).
  "Listen to your father, who gave you life, and do not despise your mother when she is old" (Proverbs 23:22).
- "May your father and mother be glad; may she who gave you birth rejoice!" (Proverbs 23:25).
- "For a son dishonors his father, a daughter rises up against her mother . . ." (Micah 7:6)
- "Anyone who loves his father or mother more than me is not worthy of me . . ." (Matthew 10:37)

Paul compares himself with a mother and a father:

- ". . . but we were gentle among you, like a mother caring for her little children. We love you so much that we were delighted to share with you not only the gospel of God but our lives as well, because you had become so dear to us" (1 Thessalonians 2:7-8).

> • "For you know that we dealt with each of you as a father deals with his own children, encouraging, comforting and urging you to live lives worthy of God, who calls you into his kingdom and glory" (1 Thessalonians 2:11-12).

2. Occasionally, the Bible mentions the child-rearing responsibility of the father towards the children without mentioning the mother (e.g., Ephesians 6:4; Isaiah 38:19; Joshua 4:21; comp. the warnings ibid. and Colossians 3:21). Surely, nowhere does it say that child-rearing is solely a matter for women. Thus, one reads: "Fathers ... bring them up in the training and instruction of the Lord" (Ephesians 6:4). How does anyone want to do that from their place of work? Expressions such as "father's household" are used 201 times in the Old Testament (Genesis 46:21; Joshua 2:18) for family. And can we think that the father is not to have anything to do with the "home"? Fatherhood means to (co-) call something into being and carry responsibility for it both internally and outwardly.

A warning about child-rearing which is either too strict or too lax

• "Fathers, do not exasperate your children; instead, bring them up in the training and instruction of the Lord" (Ephesians 6:4).
• "Fathers, do not embitter your children, or they will become discouraged" (Colossians 3:21).

Negative examples

• David spared his sons too much. Thus, the following is mentioned as a reason for Adonijah's rebellion against David, his father and king: "His father had never interfered with him by asking, 'Why do you behave as you do?'" (1 Kings 1:6).
• Eli did not have the nerve to intervene towards his sons when they abused their priestly office, for which reason God judged him along with his family (particularly 1 Samuel 2-3; 2:22-25).
• For that reason, God has to turn the hearts of the fathers to their children (Luke 1:17; Malachi 4:6 – there is also a reversal there).

Love and strictness, compassion and admonishment, obedience and role modeling are part of fatherly child-rearing. Fathers are always role models for their children! A condition of the office of elder and of overseer is, therefore, believing children: 1 Timothy 3:4-5; Titus 1:6,9. In child-rearing it is the taught and lived-out law of God which plays the decisive role:

"These commandments that I give you today are to be upon your hearts. Impress them on your children. Talk about them when you sit at home and when you walk along the road, when you lie down and when you get up" (Deuteronomy 6:6-7; similarly 11:19).

3. Man is addressed as the head in 1 Corinthians 11:3,4,7 and Ephesians 5:23; and in 1 Peter 3:1,5,6 and Ephesians 5:21-22 there is mention of the wife's being in submission or better integration. While the traditional interpretation sees a confirmation of patriarchal family circumstances, others see the placement of the husband as the representative of the family covenant and not, however, as the abolishment of marriage as a covenant between two equal individuals who are on equal footing. What in the process is decisive is the following: As far as the questions of the division of child-rearing responsibilities and the earning of a livelihood are concerned, items with practical consequences do not emerge from the Bible.

In the Bible, being the head is nowhere linked with being the provider. Instead, the wife contributes to the livelihood (e.g., Proverbs 31:10-31 speaks of being "profitable" and of the fact that the wife "provides . . . for her family" by being productive outside of the home, for instance as an entrepreneur), and nowhere in the Bible is a woman forbidden from working, and she is also not forbidden from working for money. Limiting fatherhood to the functions of earning and providing does not have a Biblical and Christian justification. Rather, it developed for the first time in the 19th century, as we have already seen.

4. *The duty the children have to obey is likewise not linked with the man's being the head. Rather, it is always related to the father and the mother.* For that matter, what is also important is that the Bible nowhere subordinates the wife and the children to the husband. Rather, it is the children who are placed in such a relationship with respect to both parents.

In the Bible, authority is otherwise *also* always linked to the authority to punish, which for instance, the father and the mother have towards the children but which the state also has towards its subjects (Romans 13:1-7). The husband also nowhere has even the hint of an authority to punish his wife. Nowhere is a call found for the husband to see to it that the wife complies, much less that he can punish her or introduce other measures against her dissenting views. The sole "weapon" the wife has is to love his wife as Christ loves the church (Ephesians 5:25). The main task of the husband is to selflessly encourage his wife and enable her to have a dignified and good life (Ephesians 5:26-29).

5. *Authority and responsibility within the Biblical work ethic bring along more work* and not less, also with respect to the parents' authority and the authority of the father. The command to work also applies to the powerful and it precisely applies to the powerful. For that reason, kings lead a particularly industrious life. And Paul, who is certainly not without influence, writes, "I worked harder than all of them" (1 Corinthians 15:10; see also 2 Corinthians 11:23). That was the price for his responsibility. In the Bible, superiors work for their subordinates just as subordinates work for their superiors. Parents work for their children. Authority in the Bible means work, whereby the highest authority, God himself, works and does more for us than we would ever be able to do for others. Parents' authority over their children does not produce a comfortable life for the parents. Rather, it produces much more activity. And that is precisely not supposed to apply to the father? The authority humankind has over the earth (Genesis 1:26 30), as the crown of creation, thus the mandate to subdue the earth, which man and woman received together, means the mandate to work, to manage the earth, indeed not only to "work it" but rather to "take care of it" (Genesis 2:15).

6. *God is the archetype and role model of each expression of fatherhood*: "For this reason I kneel before the Father, from whom his whole family in heaven and on earth derives its name" (Ephesians 3:14-15). At the same time, (good) fathers serve as examples of God (e.g., Luke 11:11-13). Trust in the Father, is for that reason the best precondition for human fatherhood: "He who fears the Lord has a secure fortress, and for his children it will be refuge" (Proverbs 14:26).

The intent is not to put forth God as a man or fatherhood as more dignified than motherhood. However, it is to take it seriously that God's fatherhood is a role model for all fathers and one by which they will be judged. Man and woman are the image of God, and God stands above all genders. The Bible also has no reservations about speaking of mothers as good examples of God (Isaiah 66:13: "As a mother comforts her child, so will I [God] comfort you; and you will be comforted over Jerusalem") even if this is more seldom. Thus, the Bible can speak about the fact that we are "born" of God (John 1:13; 1 John 3:9 and six additional times in 1 John) and that God has a "womb" (Isaiah 46:3; 66:9).

7. *God's fatherhood is also expressed in the fact that he is compassionate and he consoles.* God's fatherhood is shown precisely in the fact that he has a personal relationship with us and raises us personally in a way that is best

for us (not for others or for everyone). The father who receives the prodigal son is the role model for every father!

In addition to compassion, *faithfulness* is a particular characteristic of a good father, and a father conveys in a special way what it means that God is faithful and reliable: "... fathers tell their children about your [God's] faithfulness" (Isaiah 38:19).

Characteristics of God included in his Fatherhood and exemplary for biological and spiritual fathers

Compassion and consolation
- "As a father has compassion on his children, so the Lord has compassion on those who fear him" (Psalm 103:13).
- "Praise be to the God and Father of our Lord Jesus Christ, the Father of compassion and the God of all comfort" (2 Corinthians 1:3).
- The father in the Parable of the Prodigal son (Luke 15:11-32)
- (God about Solomon:) "I will be his father and he will be my son. When he does wrong, I will punish him ... But my love will never be taken away from him ..." (2 Samuel 7: 14-15; a balance between strictness and kindness).

Redemption and preservation
- "... you, O Lord, are our Father, our Redeemer from of old is your name" (Isaiah 63:16).
- "In the same way, your Father in heaven is not willing that any of these little ones should be lost" (Matthew 18:14).

Practicing protection and caring
- "You are my Father, my God, the Rock my Savior" (Psalm 89:27).
- "Though my father and mother forsake me, the Lord will receive me" (Psalm 27:10).
- "... a father to the fatherless, a defender of widows ..." (Psalm 68:6; comp. Psalm 10:14)

Teaching
- Comp. Deuteronomy 6:6-7; 11:19; James 1:5; Proverbs 2:1-6.

Being a role model
- "Be imitators of God, therefore, as dearly loved children ..." (Ephesians 5:1).

- "You became imitators of us and of the Lord . . ." (1 Thessalonians 1:6).

Having authority

- "A son honors his father . . . If I am a father, where is the honor due me?" (Malachi 1:6).
- (about Jesus:) For he received honor and glory from God the Father . . ." (2 Peter 1:17)

Leading

- "as I bring them back . . . because I am Israel's father . . ." (Jeremiah 31:9)

Admonishing, child-rearing, punishment

- The suffering of an individual is understood as fatherly child-rearing: Proverbs 3:12; Job 36:5; Psalm 66:10; 118:18; 119:67, 71.
- Proverbs 3:12: . . . because the Lord disciplines those he loves, as a father the son he delights in" (Proverbs 3:12; quoted in Hebrews 12:4-11).
- "Know then in your heart that as a man disciplines his son, so the Lord your God disciplines" (Deuteronomy 8:5).
- "Return, faithless people . . ." (Jeremiah 3:19, 22)
- 2 Samuel 7:14-15 (see above)

Creating

- (God creates and conceives, while a biological and spiritual father only conceives.)
- Malachi 2:10; Deuteronomy 32:6; Job 38:28; Isaiah 45:10, comp. 45:9-11

2.   Single Fathers, Stepfathers, "Ex-Fathers"

Single fathers

In the following it is not a question of making life difficult for single fathers, stepfathers, and others. However, only those who soberly recognize a possible deficit can produce a remedy and alternatives. Moves to another location, for example, are among the most stressful events for children. For that reason, one should think twice about doing this during the phase when you have children. However, if it is unavoidable, then ignoring the situation is of no help. Rather, actively processing this is the only answer. There has to be a lot of talking before and after and ways to ease the upheavals within their trusted living environment. Fatherlessness or raising a child alone has similar consequences which are not solved by angrily declaring them to be non-existent. Rather, it is done by taking a lot of time for children, getting your own ideas, collecting ideas with others, and actively counteracting typical problems.

There are more than 300,000 single fathers in Germany. It is the fastest growing family form. However, along with single mothers, it is often hardly mentioned publicly for reasons of "political correctness." This is the case, although in the meantime they make up 20% of all single parents. In about 75% of all cases, a single father is the result of a divorce or separation, and in about 15% of all cases it is a matter of the death of the female partner. In less than 10% of all cases the man had always been single or had only a loose relationship with a woman.

Most single fathers have already demonstrated an above average level of activity in the household. They come from all levels of society, since this way of life is seldom chosen consciously. Single fathers are mostly better off due to their profession than single mothers. However, the threat of unemployment is a great challenge, especially since only one out of five mothers pays support for the children of single fathers.

In somewhat more than one-half of divorce cases, the ruling is consensually agreed upon that the children grow up with the father, while in something less than one-half of the cases the request on the part of the mother is not granted on account of alcoholism, drugs, psychological illness, or child neglect.

Even if it is the case that the fewest number of single fathers want this situation to be a permanent condition, in most cases it is a permanent way of life. This means that despite principally being open for a new partnership, there is mostly no new partner who comes into question as a stepmother.

Single fathers can be successful.[97] Whoever has understood that a father and a mother are equally important for the rearing of children also understands that a single father indeed has other deficits than a single mother. However, they are not more serious deficits. Single fatherhood is not easier or more difficult than single motherhood, and fathers as well as mothers can – and this has been shown by many studies – successfully take on an astonishingly great number of tasks when the husband or the wife needs to do so.

Since 1998, when new legislation was passed governing the rights of the child in Germany, there has fortunately been the following in § 1626 (3) of the German Civil Code:

"The best interests of the child as a general rule include contact with both parents." This also puts Article 9 of the Convention on the Rights of the Child into practice, which was accepted in 1989 by the General Assembly of the United Nations and has applied in Germany since 1992. Therein, the right to live with both parents is among the rights of a child. This is a good thing, and it also applies as much as possible after a divorce.

Recommendations for single fathers and divorced fathers

- Make sure that your children have a good picture of their biological mother in their mind or retain such a memory. Tell them about the good days from the time of pregnancy and birth.
- Convey clearly to your children that they are not guilty and that this mistake lies between the adults. Do not make allies out of the children.
- Make sure that your children have at least one woman as a role model in their life whom they truly get to know, be it a relative (e.g., an aunt, a grandmother), teacher, church worker, or a long-standing female friend.
- Take everything to heart that is recommended to single mothers in the following. As far as is possible after a divorce, make sure there are good rights of access granted to the biological mother.

Recommendations for single mothers and divorced mothers

I am making an exception to speak to mothers here, because in 80% of all cases it is the mother who files for divorce.[98] After that, it is mostly the mother who decides which type of contact to the biological father the children will have. Naturally, all of this can also apply to the father when they are in charge of the child or the children after a divorce.

- If the child is not directly threatened by the father (e.g., violence, sexual abuse), do not alienate the child from his or her biological father. Your child does not have the least to do with what occurs between your partner and you or what is still occurring. Strictly separate your feelings for your ex-husband from your care for the child and the feelings the child has for his or her father.

- Always speak positively about the time when the three of you lived together. Unload your bitterness about the past with other adults.
- When you have to mention certain negative actions on the part of your ex-husband, make sure that it is a question of clearly outlined and documented actions which the children can understand. Avoid demonizing or giving a fundamentally negative depiction of the character of your ex-husband.
- Your child is not your psychiatrist from whom you want to get advice. Your child is not your judge, before whom you have to justify yourself. Your child is not your mother or friend, to whom you go to have a cry. Your child needs trust, warmth, protection, leadership, and counseling. When you speak about family affairs and the ex-husband, speak about the life and identity of the child because for the child even the worst father will always remain his or her father.

Stepfathers

Stepfathers have long since become a part of everyday life in our time. The central problem is "that up to just a few decades ago, the role of the stepfather in our cultural environment was relatively clearly defined. He had to replace the deceased father as the head of the family, as the child-rearer of the family, and in many cases as the provider for the children. The fact that becoming a stepfather is in many cases preceded by a divorce or a separation between the biological parents and the fact that the stepfather comes along in addition to the biological father who is still alive, as well as due to circumstances where the role of the father has been subject to massive changes over past decades, have all led to the role of the stepfather being an extremely indefinable one. There is no generally valid or institutionally expected role for the stepfather. He does not possess any rights and duties towards his stepchildren, and he is not related to them. It is unclear as to the degree he replaces the father who lives outside of the family, whether he should be the child-rearer, a leisure time buddy, a good friend, or only the mother's partner. It is often expected that he is at the same time a parent and a 'non-parent' Thus the biological mother mostly expects that the stepfather be integrated into the family, that he take on the tasks of a father, and that he relieve her in providing care and participating in the upbringing. At the same time, mothers often react in a contradictory manner when their partners behave in a manner corresponding to these expectations. Indeed, many mothers often want support and relief with respect to the children, but they are not prepared to give up a part of their upbringing competence and responsibility ... Also, the expectations and desires the children have with respect to the 'new' man in the family can be extremely different and sometimes contradictory. They can range from the hope of getting the 'right' father, to the expectation of having gained a leisure time buddy, a chum, or a good friend, and on to the desire that this man will not interfere in the affairs of the family and that he will again be gone from the family as quickly as possible. In light of these ambiguities, it is not surprising that stepfathers often evaluate themselves worse than biological fathers, that they entertain doubts, and face their own role self-critically ..."[99]

On the other hand, stepfathers also have great opportunities, since loving and determined men who have time, can be esteemed by children, and stepfathers can be true companions for life. Children like having exemplary men in their life, and most of the time stepfathers remain the only men playing a shaping role in the life of the children.

It is thus tremendously important for stepfathers to discuss in detail with the mother what roles they are to play and to then convey this clearly to the children. Should they replace the biological father with all his rights and duties? Should they only be a good friend of the family and not question the role of the biological father, etc.? Children can adjust to an astonishingly large number of situations and rules. There is only one thing which they do poorly: constantly see the rules changed and thus grow up in uncertainty.

If one asks which factors, seen statistically, help stepfathers form a positive relationship with their children, these are 1. one's own biological children, 2. being married to the mother, 3. having a harmonious permanent relationship with the mother, 4. the expressed desire of the mother that the stepfather assume full rights and duties, 5. mutual values of upbringing held by the father and the mother, 6. the age of the children – the older they are, the more difficult it is for them to accept the new father. If the first father has died, the stepfather is mostly accepted rather easily. If the first father is still living and is only no longer present in the family due to divorce, being a stepfather is a significantly greater challenge.

Recommendations for stepfathers

- Agree upon with the mother which of the many different possible roles you should have and want as a stepfather, and take a consistent stand for holding to this agreement and not changing your role daily according to the situation or mood.
- Make sure that when the family meets it is clearly communicated to the children which tasks they have and what their rights and duties are and are not.
- It is absolutely important to consider adoption if the biological father is no longer living or is completely unknown to the child. However, if the biological father is still living and the child regularly sees him, you should not create a legal situation where an appearance is conveyed to the child that you want to cut out the child's biological father.

III. Literature Tips

The Importance of Fathers and Families and the Dangers of Fatherlessness

https://www.fatherly.com/health-science/science-benefits-of-fatherhood-dads-father-effect/

https://www.focusonthefamily.com/socialissues/marriage/high-cost-of-fatherlessness/high-cost-to-fatherlessness-to-children

http://fathers.com/statistics-and-research/the-consequences-of-fatherlessness/ (2019)

https://mensrights.com.au/hot-topics/the-high-costs-of-fatherlessness/ (2019)

https://www.psychologytoday.com/us/blog/the-time-cure/201808/the-fatherless-generation (2018)

https://www.ncbi.nlm.nih.gov/pmc/articles/PMC3904543/ (2013)

http://www.fira.ca/cms/documents/29/Effects_of_Father_Involvement.pdf (2007)

http://www.ecdip.org/docs/pdf/IF%20Father%20Res%20Summary%20%28KD%29.pdf (2002)

Meg Meeker. *Strong Fathers, Strong Daughters*. Regnery: Washington, 2007

Kyle D. Pruett, *Fatherneed: Why Father Care is as Essential as Mother Care for Your Child*, New York: Broadway Books, 2000.

Pamela Thomas. *Fatherless Daughters: Turning the Pain of Loss into the Power of Forgiveness*. Simon & Schuster: New York, 2018

Babul Luise. The Fatherless Daughter Project: Understanding Our Losses and Reclaiming Our Lives. Penguin Random House, New York City, 2016

David Blankenhorn. *Fatherless America: Confronting Our Most Urgent Social Problem*. HarperCollins: Neww York City, 1996

Sam Mehaffie, Darlene Mehaffie. *Fatherless America and the Church*. Createspace Independent Pub, n. pl., 2014

John A. Sowers, Donald Miller. *Fatherless Generation: Redeeming the Story*. Zondervan: Grand Rapids (MI), 2010

Jonathan Diamond. *Fatherless Sons. Healing the Legacy of Loss.* John Wiley & Sons: New York City, 2006

David Popenoe. *Families Without Fathers.* Aldine Transaction: New Brunswick, 2009

David Popenoe, *Life without Father: Compelling New Evidence that Fatherhood and Marriage are Indispensable for the Good of Children and Society*, New York: Free Press, 1996.

Marybeth Shinn, "Father Absence and Children's Cognitive Development," *Psychological Bulletin* 85 (1978), pp. 295-324.

Louis Kriesberg. *Mothers in Poverty A Study of Fatherless Families.* Aldine Transaction: New Brunswick, 2006

In German:

Facetten der Vaterschaft. Berlin, Bundesministerium für Familie, Senioren, Frauen und Jugend, 2006. 250 pp. (mainly by Wassilios E. Fthenakis and colleagues), only electronically: www.bmfsfj.de/Kategorien/ Forschungsnetz/forschungsberichte,did=70116.html.

Franz-Xaver Kaufmann, *Schrumpfende Gesellschaft: Vom Bevölkerungsrückgang und seinen Folgen*, Frankfurt: Suhrkamp, 2005.

Dieter Lenzen, *Vaterschaft: Vom Patriarchat zur Alimentation*, Reinbek: Rowohlt Taschenbuch Verlag, 1991 (Original date of publication)/2002.

Frank Pittman, *Warum Söhne ihre Väter brauchen: Der schwierige Weg zur Männlichkeit*, München: dtv, 1996.

Thomas Schirrmacher, *Der Segen von Ehe und Familie*, Bonn: Verlag für Kultur und Wissenschaft, 2006.

Matthias Franz, among others, "Wenn der Vater fehlt: Epidemiologische Befunde zur Bedeutung früher Abwesenheit des Vaters für die psychische Gesundheit im späteren Leben," Zeitschrift für psychosomatische Medizin 45 (1999), pp. 260-278 (abridged version in Psychologie heute 3/2004: www.vafk.de/themen/wissen/psycho/ wenn_der_vater_fehlt.htm).

Ellen Frauenknecht, "Der Schlüssel zum Glück: geteilte Kinder-Erziehung," Die Welt, May 30, 1998, p. G10.

Horst Petri, "Vaterlose Gesellen: Es wird höchste Zeit zu erkennen, welche Katastrophe für die Gesellschaft in der Vaterlosigkeit steckt," Die Welt, April 19, 2000, p. 11.

Ulrike Plewina, "Das Trauma der Trennung: Wenn Mama und Papa auseinandergehen, leiden die Kinder oft ein Leben lang," Focus 49/2001, pp. 52-65.

Paul Josef Cordes, *Die verlorenen Väter: Ein Notruf*, Freiburg: Herder, 2003.

Matthias Franz, "Wenn der Vater fehlt – Spätfolgen einer vaterlosen Gesellschaft," pp. 167-182 in: Eberhard Beckers, among others, Die Programmierung des kindlichen und jugendlichen Gehirns, Gießen: Verlag des Professorenforums, 2002.

Michiaki und Hildegard Horie, Auf der Suche nach dem verlorenen Vater, Wuppertal: R. Brockhaus, 1989[2].

Horst Petri, Das Drama der Vaterentbehrung: Chaos der Gefühle – Kräfte der Heilung, Freiburg: Herder, 2000[2] (not used here: 2006[3]).

Thomas Schirrmacher, Der Segen von Ehe und Familie, pp. 74-82, 116-124 (see above).

Alexander Thomas, "Untersuchungen zum Problem der vaterlosen Erziehung in ihrem Einfluß auf die psycho-soziale Entwicklung des Kindes," *Psychologische Beiträge* 22 (1980), pp. 27-48.

Father Research

http://thefatheringproject.org/research/

https://aleteia.org/2017/06/30/the-research-is-in-fathers-are-irreplaceable/

http://www.fatherhoodinstitute.org

https://www.fatherhood.org/fatherhood-research

http://www.fathers.com/statistics-and-research/

http://www.fira.ca

https://www.fatherly.com/health-science/science-benefits-of-fatherhood-dads-father-effect/

http://www.fatherhoodinstitute.org/2018/contemporary-fathers-in-the-uk/

https://www.frpn.org

Henry B. Biller, Fathers and Families. Paternal Factors in Child Development, Westport (CT, USA)/London: Auburn House, 1993.

Henry B. Biller/Richard S. Solomon, Child Maltreatment and Paternal Deprivation, Lexington (MA, USA)/ Toronto: Lexington Books, 1986.

Henry B. Biller, Paternal Deprivation, Lexington (MA, USA): Heath, 1974.

Natasha Cabrera, Catherine S. Tamis-LeMonda, Robert H. Bradley, Sandra Hofferth, Michael E. Lamb, "Fatherhood in the Twenty-First Century," Child Development 71 (2000), pp. 127-136.

Michael E. Lamb (ed.), The Role of the Father in Child Development, New York: John Wiley & Sons 1976[1]; 1981[2]; 1997[3]; 2004[4] (the respective editions are significantly expanded and updated).

Michael E. Lamb/Charlie Lewis, "The Development and Significance of Father-Child Relationships in Two-Parent Families," pp. 272-306, in: Michael E. Lamb (ed.), The Role of the Father in Child Development, New York: John Wiley & Sons 2004[4].

Margaret O'Brien, "Social Science and Public Policy Perspectives on Fatherhood in the European Union", pp. 121-145, in: Michael E. Lamb (ed.), The Role of the Father in Child Development, New York: John Wiley & Sons 2004[4].

In German:

Stephan Barth, "Vaterschaft im Wandel." www.stephan-barth.de/vater sch.htm.

"Das neue Bild vom Vater," Geo 1/2001. www.geo.de/GEO/kultur/gesell schaft/780.html?p=1.

Judith Rauch, "Das neue Bild vom Vater." Spiegel Online, April 25, 2006. www.spiegel.de/wissenschaft/mensch/0,1518,411244,00.html.

Christine Brinck, "Familie ist nicht gleich Familie," Die Welt, March 15, 2000, p. 11.

Jean Le Camus, Väter: die Bedeutung des Vaters für die psychische Entwicklung des Kindes, Weinheim: Beltz, 2001, 2003.

Jean Le Camus, Vater sein heute: für eine neue Vaterrolle, Weinheim: Beltz, 2001.

Horst Petri, Väter sind anders: Die Bedeutung der Vaterrolle für den Mann, Stuttgart: Kreuz, 2004.

Ursula Lehr, "Die Rolle von Vater und Mutter in der frühen Sozialisation des Kindes." Therapiewoche 30 (1980), pp. 649-665.

Wassilios E. Fthenakis, among others, Engagierte Vaterschaft, Opladen: Leske und Budrich, 1999.

Wassilios E. Fthenakis, Väter, 2 Vols., München: Urban und Schwarzenberg, 1985; München: dtv, 1988.

Wassilios E. Fthenakis/Beate Minsel. Die Rolle des Vaters in der Familie. Schriftenreihe des Bundesministeriums für Familie, Senioren, Frauen und Jugend 213, Stuttgart: W. Kohlhammer, 2002.

Karin Grossmann/Klaus E. Grossmann, Bindungen – das Gefüge psychischer Sicherheit, Stuttgart: Klett-Cotta 2004 (additionally: Katrin Sachse. "Der geheimnisvolle Code," Focus 38/2004, pp. 124-132).

Inge Seiffke-Krenke, Psychotherapie und Entwicklungspsychologie, Berlin/Heidelberg: Springer, 2004, Chapter 7, pp. 195-224.

Inge Seiffke-Krenke. "Neuere Ergebnisse der Vaterforschung." Psychotherapeut 46 (2001) 6, pp. 391-397.

Practical Tips for "Expectant Fathers;" Advice for Phases of Development

https://www.parents.com/parenting/dads/101/how-life-changes-when-you-become-a-dad/

https://kidshealth.org/en/parents/father.html

https://www.verywellfamily.com/ways-becoming-a-dad-changes-you-1270648

https://www.gq.com/story/how-to-be-a-father

http://www.hackingfatherhoodbook.com

Ken Canfield, *The Heart of a Father: How Dads can Shape the Destiny of America*, Chicago: Northfield, 1996.

Nate Dallas. *Hacking Fatherhood: Preparing for Success in the Biggest Role of Your Life*. Nathan Dallas: New York, 2017

Armin A. Brott. *The New Father: A Dad's Guide to the First Year*. Abbeville: New York, 2015-7th ed.

Armin A. Brott. *The Expectant Father: The Ultimate Guide for Dads-to-Be*. Abbeville: New York, 2015-4th ed.

Tom Limbert. *Dad's Playbook*. Chronicle Books: San Francisco, 2012

Larry Hagner. *The Dad's Edge*. Larry Hagner, USA. 2015, Download: https://www.orderofman.com/wp-content/uploads/2016/07/Dads-Edge-for-Chris.pdf

Gary Greenberg, Jeannie Hayden. Be Prepared: A Practical Handbook for New Dads. Simon & Schuster: New York, 2004

Nate Dallas. Hacking Fatherhood. Nate Dallas: USA, 2017

In German:

www.familienhandbuch.de.

Ian Banks, Vater sein dagegen sehr: Kluger Rat für werdende und erziehende Väter und ihre Partnerinnen, Zürich: Oesch, 2003.

Lothar Beyer, Das Baby-Buch für neue Väter, München: Mosaik/Ullstein, 2005.

Wassilios E. Fthenakis/Martin R. Textor (eds.), Knaurs Handbuch Familie, München: Knaur, 2004.

Harry H. Harrison, Vater & Sohn, Hamburg: Lardon Media, 2004.

Harry H. Harrison, Vater & Tochter, Hamburg: Lardon Media, 2004.

Jens Oenicke, Der werdende Vater – Anleitung zur perfekten Vaterschaft, Berlin: Zeitgeistfactory, 2005.

Jan-Uwe Rogge, Kinder brauchen Grenzen, Reinbek: Rowohlt Taschenbuch Verlag, 2004[25]; Kinder brauchen Grenzen. Eltern setzen Grenzen, ibid. 2007.

Robert Richter/Eberhard Schäfer, Das Papa-Handbuch: Alles, was Sie wissen müssen zu Schwangerschaft, Geburt und dem ersten Jahr zu dritt, München: Gräfe und Unzer, 2005.

Felix Rohner-Dobler, Familien brauchen Väter: Ermutigung und Rituale, München: Kösel, 2006.

Ralf Ruhl, Kinder machen Männer stark: Vater werden, Vater sein, Reinbek: Rowohlt Taschenbuch Verlag, 2000.

Christian Guidebooks and Aids, Research on Christian Families

Rick Johnsone. *Better Dads, Stronger Sons*. Fleming H. Revell: Acta (MI), 2017

Traci Smith. *Faithful Families*. Chalice Press: Atlanta (GA), 2017

W. Bradford Wilcox, *Soft Patriarchs, New Men: How Christianity Shapes Fathers and Husbands*, Chicago/London: The University of Chicago Press, 2004.

Etan Thomas, Nick Chiles (ed). *Fatherhood*. Penguin: New York, 2013

In German:

James Dobson, Das eigenwillige Kind, Holzgerlingen: Hänssler, 2001[4].

James Dobson, Anti-Frust-Buch für Eltern von willigen und eigenwilligen Kindern, Kehl: Edition Trobisch, 1993[2].

James Dobson, Der große Familien- und Erziehungsratgeber, Holzgerlingen: Hänssler, 1998.

James Dobson/Shirley Dobson, Stille Zeit für Eltern: Andachten zum Auftanken, Asslar: Gerth, 2005[2].

Wilhelm Faix, Wie viel Vater braucht ein Kind? Holzgerlingen: Hänssler, 2003.

Wilhelm Faix, Die christliche Familie heute: Ergebnisse einer Untersuchung, Bonn: VKW, 2000.

Michiaki und Hildegard Horie, Auf der Suche nach dem verlorenen Vater, Wuppertal: R. Brockhaus, 1989[2].

Cornelia Mack/Friedhilde Stricker (eds.), Zum Leben erziehen, Hänssler: Holzgerlingen, 2002, therein by Thomas Schirrmacher: "Die Ehe der Eltern," pp. 101-107 and "Generationen und unterschiedliche Erziehungsmaßstäbe," pp. 182-187.

Eberhard Mühlan, Bleib cool, Papa! Guter Rat für gestreßte Väter, Asslar: Gerth, 2001[4].

Thomas Schirrmacher, Erziehung, Bildung, Schule, VTR: Nürnberg, 2002.

Thomas Schirrmacher, Ethik, 7 Vols., Hamburg: RVB/Nürnberg: VTR, 2004[3], Vol. 4.

Hermann J. Zoche, Vorbilder prägen Weltbilder: Kleinkinder mit christlichen Werten erziehen, Augsburg: Sankt Ulrich, 2002.

Compatibility of Fatherhood /Parenthood and Career

Josh Levs. All in: How Our Work-First Culture Fails Dads, Families, and Businesses--And How We Can Fix It Together. HarperOne: New York, 2015

Neil Sinclair. Commando Dad: Mission Adventure: Get Active with Your Kids. Summersdale Publishers: Chister (UK), 2016

In German:

Projekt "Balance von Familie und Arbeitswelt" on the following websites: www.bmfsfj.de and www.bertelsmann-stiftung.de.

Consuelo Gräfin Ballestrem, *Familie contra Beruf?*, Augsburg: Sankt Ulrich 2002

Werner *Eichhorst*, among others, *Vereinbarkeit von Familie und Beruf im internationalen Vergleich*, Gütersloh: Verlag Bertelsmann Stiftung 2007.

Günter F. Gross, *Beruflich Profi, privat Amateur? Berufliche Spitzenleistungen und persönliche Lebensqualität*, Landsberg: verlag moderne industrie 1989[1]; 2005[19].

Liz Mohn/Ursula von der Leyen (eds.), *Familie gewinnt*, Gütersloh: Verlag Bertelsmann Stiftung 2007.

Fathers and Divorce

https://www.fatherly.com/health-science/psychological-effects-divorce-fathers-men-suicide/

Paul R. Amato/Julie M. Sobolewski, "The Effects of Divorce on Fathers and and Children: Nonresidential Fathers and Stephfathers," pp. 341-367 in: Michael E. Lamb (ed.), *The Role of the Father in Child Development*, New York: John Wiley & Sons 2004[4].

Robert E. Emery. *The Truth About Children and Divorce: Dealing with the Emotions So You and Your Children Can Thrive.* Penguin: New York, 2006

Robert E. Emery. *Coping With Divorce, Single Parenting, and Remarriage: A Risk and Resiliency Perspective.* Psychology Press: London, 2014

Robert E. Emery. *Cultural Sociology of Divorce: An Encyclopedia.* Sage Publications: London, 2013

JoAnne Pedro-Carroli. *Putting the Children First: Proven Stragegies for Helping Children Thrive Through Divorce.* Avedry: New York, 2010

In German:

Das Kindschaftsrecht. Berlin: Bundesministerium der Justiz 2003, auch unter http://www.bmj.de/files/-/739/DasKindschaftsrecht.pdf.

Gerhard Amendt, "Väterlichkeit, Scheidung und Geschlechterkampf," Aus Politik und Zeitgeschehen (2004) 19, pp. 19-25 – www.vafk.de/themen/aktuell/news/bpb-2004-19-A.html   or www.bundestag.de/dasparlament/2004/19/Beilage/003.html.

Gerhard Amendt, Scheidungsväter. Bremen: Institut für Geschlechter- und Generationenforschung 2004; erweitert: Frankfurt am Main: Campus 2006.

Lu Decurtins/Peter C. Meyer (ed.), Entschieden geschieden: Was Trennung und Scheidung für Väter bedeutet, Zürich: Verlag Rüegger 2001.

Fthenakis/Textor, Knaurs Handbuch Familie, pp. 430-473 (see above).

Matthias Matussek, Die vaterlose Gesellschaft, Reinbek: Rowohlt Taschenbuch Verlag 1998; updated: Frankfurt: Fischer Taschenbuch Verlag 2006.

Anneke Napp-Peters, Ein-Elternteil-Familie: Soziale Randgruppe oder neues familiales Selbstverständnis?, Weinheim und München: Juventa 1987[2] (1985[1]).

Anneke Napp-Peters, Scheidungsfamilien: Interaktionsmuster und kindliche Entwicklung, Frankfurt: Eigenverlag des Deutschen Vereins für öffentliche und private Fürsorge 1988.

Thomas Schirrmacher, Der Segen von Ehe und Familie, pp. 82-110 (see above).

Stepfathers

https://www.ncbi.nlm.nih.gov/pmc/articles/PMC5159685/

https://www.fatherly.com/health-science/science-how-to-be-good-stepfather-stepdads/

https://onlinelibrary.wiley.com/doi/pdf/10.1111/j.1545-5300.1979.00175.x

Ron L. Deal. The Smart Stepdad: Steps to Help You Succeed. Bethany House: Bloomigton (MN), 2011

Ron L. Deal. The Smart Stepfamily. Bethany House: Bloomigton (MN), 2014

Matthew Massimo. Stepparenting. Amazon: USA, 2014

Amato/Sobolewski, "Stepfathers," pp. 356-359 (see above)

In German:

Facetten der Vaterschaft, pp. 118-125 (see above).

Fthenakis/Textor, Knaurs Handbuch Familie, pp. 490-497 (see above).

Schirrmacher, Der Segen von Ehe und Familie, pp. 110-116 (see above).

Liselotte Wilk, "Die Gestaltung multipler Vaterschaft in Stieffamilien," pp. 121-142 in: Sabine Walper/Beate Schwarz (eds.), Was wird aus den Kindern? Chancen und Risiken für die Entwicklung aus Trennungs- *und Stieffamilien*, Weinheim: Juventa 2002[2].

Differences between Men and Women; Being a Man

https://www.marsvenus.com

Twelve books by John Gray on 'Mars' and 'venus', see https://www.marsvenus.com/list/john-gray-mars-venus-books

Anne Moir/David Jessel, Brainsex: The Real Difference between Men and Women. New York: Delta, 1992

Larry Crab. Men and Women: Enjoying the Differences. Grand Rapoids (MI): Zondervan, 2013

In German:

Rolf Degen, "Kleine Differenzen: Auch im Gehirn unterscheiden sich Frau und Mann." *Bild der Wissenschaft* (1992) 10, pp. 24-27.0

Christof Gaspari, *Eins plus eins ist eins: Leitbilder für Mann und Frau*, Wien: Herold Verlag, 1985.

John Gray, *Männer sind anders. Frauen auch*, München: Goldmann, 2002.

John Gray, *Mars, Venus und Partnerschaft: Vertrautheit, Nähe und Liebe durch offene Kommunikation*, Rheda-Wiedenbrück: RM-Buch, 1999.

Anne Moir/David Jessel, *Brainsex: Der wahre Unterschied zwischen Mann und Frau*, Düsseldorf: Econ 1990[1]; 1996[3].

Paul M. Zulehner/Rainer Volz, *Männer im Aufbruch*, Ostfildern: Schwabenverlag, 1999[3].

Endnoten

1   Annette Zinkant, *Mr. Unentschieden: Warum Männer zu nichts taugen*, Frankfurt: Krüger, 2006².

2   Cordes, *Die verlorenen Väter*, p. 9. Full information about materials in footnotes is found in the literature tips at the end of the book.

3   Petri, "Vaterlose Gesellen," p. 11.

4   Everything according to *Die Welt*, May 18, 2007, p. 4.

5   Rohner-Dobler, *Familien brauchen Väter*, p. 29.

6   Banks, *Vater sein dagegen sehr . . .*, p. 14.

7   Op. cit., p. 11.

8   Op. cit.

9   Reprint by Thomas Schirrmacher, "Papa & Co.": *Neues Leben 44* (1999), p. 9.

10   On the historical development see Lenzen, *Vaterschaft*, und in a short form: *Facetten der Vaterschaft*, pp. 6-15.

11   Barth, "Vaterschaft im Wandel."

12   *Facetten der Vaterschaft*, p. 9.

13   See Rogge, *Kinder brauchen Grenzen*.

14   Lamb, *The Role of the Father in Child Development*, p. 27.

15   Biller/Solomon, *Child Maltreatment and Paternal Deprivation*, p. 67.

16   Lamb, op. cit., p. 29.

17   Lamb, op. cit., p. 15.

18   Pruett, *Fatherneed*.

19   Op. cit., p. 2.

20   See Rauch, "Das neue Bild vom Vater," and the studies mentioned there.

21   "Das neue Bild vom Vater," *GEO*.

22   Wassilios E. Fthenakis, *Väter*, in part. Vol. 1, pp. 23-48; pp. 209-283.

23   *Facetten der Vaterschaft*, p. 30; comp. Le Camus, *Väter*, pp. 76-81.

24   Grossmann, *Bindungen*, p. 243.

25   Research by Lorenz was already refuted in 1975 in: Gunter Pilz/Hugo Moesch (eds.), *Der Mensch und die Graugans: Eine Kritik an Konrad Lorenz*, Frankfurt: Umschau, 1975.

26   E. g., Grossmann, *Bindungen*, pp. 68; 102; 218-239.

27   See Rauch, "Das neue Bild vom Vater," and the examples mentioned there.

28   Lamb, *Role*, pp. 9-10; comp. Seiffke-Krenke, *Psychotherapie und Entwicklungspsychologie*, pp. 199-200; 220-224.

29   Barth. "Vaterschaft im Wandel" with reference to Lenzen, *Vaterschaft*.

30   Petri, *Das Drama der Vaterentbehrung*, p. 11.

31   George A. Akerlof, "Men without Children," *The Economic Journal 108* (1998), pp. 287-309.

32   Op. cit., pp. 296-297.

33   Op. cit., pp. 303.

34   Op. cit., p. 11; comp. Le Camus, *Väter*, pp. 113-128.

35   Petri, *Väter sind anders.*

36   Samuel Osheron, *Finding our Fathers*, p. 6.

37   Petri, "Vaterlose Gesellen," p. 11.

38   Biller, *Fathers and Families*, p. 3.

39   Thomas, "Untersuchungen zum Problem der vaterlosen Erziehung . . .," p. 27.

40   Petri, *Das Drama der Vaterentbehrung*, p. 158.

41   Plewina, "Das Trauma der Trennung," p. 58.

42   Franz, "Wenn der Vater fehlt" (1999).

43   Franz, "Wenn der Vater fehlt – Spätfolgen einer vaterlosen Gesellschaft" (2002).

44   Op. cit., p. 180.

45   Matussek, *Die vaterlose Gesellschaft*, p. 125. I have checked all sources mentioned there.

46   Petri, *Das Drama der Vaterentbehrung.*

47   Op. cit., p. 159.

48   Lamb, *The Role of the Father in Child Development* (2004[4]), pp. 163-164.

49   Frauenknecht, "Der Schlüssel zum Glück: geteilte Kinder-Erziehung," Research results based on a study by Yale University over a period of more than 12 years.

50   *Facetten der Vaterschaft*, p. 144.

51   Schirrmacher, *Der Segen von Ehe und Familie*, pp. 72-74.

52   Biller/Solomon, *Child Maltreatment and Paternal Deprivation*, p. 67.

53   Op. cit., p. 67.

54   Op. cit., p. 133

55   See also Schirrmacher, *Ethik*, Bd. 4, pp. 435-495.

56   Biller/Solomon, Op. cit., p. 59.

57   See more detail in Schirrmacher, *Der Segen von Ehe und Familie*, pp. 67-72.

58   Cordes, *Die verlorenen Väter*, p. 13.

59   Op. cit.

60   Thomas, "Untersuchungen zum Problem der vaterlosen Erziehung . . .," p. 35.

61   Horie, *Auf der Suche nach dem verlorenen Vater*, p. 63.

62   Both Ruhl, *Kinder machen Männer stark*, p. 101.

63   Petri, *Das Drama der Vaterentbehrung*, pp. 31-32.

64   Le Camus, *Väter*; Le Camus, *Vater sein heute.*

65   Fthenakis, *Engagierte Vaterschaft*, p. 38.

66   *Facetten der Vaterschaft*, p. 244.

67 Pruett, *Fatherneed*, pp. 7-8.
68 Beyer, *Das Baby-Buch für neue Väter*, pp. 22-23.
69 "Das neue Bild vom Vater," *GEO*; comp. Le Camus, *Väter*, pp. 46-74; pp. 91-93.
70 "Das neue Bild vom Vater," *GEO*, introductory paragraphs.
71 *Facetten der Vaterschaft*, p. 146.
72 See, for instance, the studies introduced in Grossmann, *Bindungen*, p. 529.
73 E.g., Grossmann, *Bindungen*, pp. 223-224 and *Seiffke-Krenke, Psychotherapie und Entwicklungspsychologie*, pp. 195-224.
74 Seiffke-Krenke, "Neuere Ergebnisse der Vaterforschung," pp. 392-395, and Seiffke-Krenke, *Psychotherapie und Entwicklungspsychologie*, pp. 195-224.
75 Biller, *Fathers and Families*, p. 3.
76 See in part Zoche, *Vorbilder prägen Weltbilder*.
77 Fthenakis/Textor, *Knaurs Handbuch Familie*, p. 193.
78 Moir/Jessel, *Brainsex*, comp. the studies introduced in Degen, "Kleine Differenzen."
79 Moir/Jessel, *Brainsex*, publisher advertising.
80 See Lamb/ Lewis, "The Development and Significance of Father-Child Relationships . . .", in part. pp. 272.
81 Biller, *Fathers and Families*, p. 47.
82 Fthenakis/ Textor. *Knaurs Handbuch Familie*, pp. 191-193.
83 Biller/Solomon, *Child Maltreatment and Paternal Deprivation*, p. 74.
84 Grossmann, *Bindungen*, p. 231.
85 Rohner-Dobler, *Familien brauchen Väter*, p. 103.
86 Fthenakis, *Engagierte Vaterschaft*, p. 38.
87 *Facetten der Vaterschaft*, p. 196.
88 "Das neue Bild vom Vater," *GEO*.
89 *Facetten der Vaterschaft*, pp. 69-75.
90 Kaufmann, *Schrumpfende Gesellschaft*, p. 152.
91 Op. cit., p. 153.
92 Mohn/von der Leyen, *Familie gewinnt*, p. 87, see in detail in the literature list.
93 Op. cit., p. 72.
94 Op. cit., pp. 123-124.
95 Comp. Thomas Schirrmacher, *Die neue Unterschicht*, Holzgerlingen: Hänssler, 2007.
96 See in part Mohn/von der Leyen, *Familie gewinnt*, pp. 132-133.
97 See above all: *Facetten der Vaterschaft*, pp. 103-109.
98 According to studies by Gerhard Amendt, "Väterlichkeit . . .," p. 23.
99 Wilk, "Die Gestaltung multipler Vaterschaft in Stieffamilien," pp. 124-125.